Amazon Web Services AWS Complete Self-Assessment Guide

The guidance in this Self-Assessment is based on Amazon Web Services AWS best practices and standards in business process architecture, design and quality management. The guidance is also based on the professional judgment of the individual collaborators listed in the Acknowledgments.

Notice of rights

You are licensed to use the Self-Assessment contents in your presentations and materials for internal use and customers without asking us - we are here to help.

All rights reserved for the book itself: this book may not be reproduced or transmitted in any form by any means, electronic, mechanical, photocopying, recording, or otherwise, without the prior written permission of the publisher.

The information in this book is distributed on an "As Is" basis without warranty. While every precaution has been taken in the preparation of he book, neither the author nor the publisher shall have any liability to any person or entity with respect to any loss or damage caused or alleged to be caused directly or indirectly by the instructions contained in this book or by the products described in it.

Trademarks

Many of the designations used by manufacturers and sellers to distinguish their products are claimed as trademarks. Where those designations appear in this book, and the publisher was aware of a trademark claim, the designations appear as requested by the owner of the trademark. All other product names and services identified throughout this book are used in editorial fashion only and for the benefit of such companies with no intention of infringement of the trademark. No such use, or the use of any trade name, is intended to convey endorsement or other affiliation with this book.

Copyright © by The Art of Service
http://theartofservice.com
service@theartofservice.com

Table of Contents

About The Art of Service   8
Acknowledgments   9
Included Resources - how to access   9

Your feedback is invaluable to us   11
Purpose of this Self-Assessment   11
How to use the Self-Assessment   12
Amazon Web Services AWS
Scorecard Example   14

Amazon Web Services AWS
Scorecard   15

BEGINNING OF THE
SELF-ASSESSMENT: 16
CRITERION #1: RECOGNIZE   17

CRITERION #2: DEFINE: 24

CRITERION #3: MEASURE: 35

CRITERION #4: ANALYZE: 48

CRITERION #5: IMPROVE: 57

CRITERION #6: CONTROL: 69

CRITERION #7: SUSTAIN: 80
Amazon Web Services AWS and Managing Projects, Criteria
for Project Managers: 105
1.0 Initiating Process Group: Amazon Web Services AWS 106

1.1 Project Charter: Amazon Web Services AWS   108

1.2 Stakeholder Register: Amazon Web Services AWS   110

1.3 Stakeholder Analysis Matrix: Amazon Web Services AWS
111

2.0 Planning Process Group: Amazon Web Services AWS   113

2.1 Project Management Plan: Amazon Web Services AWS
115

2.2 Scope Management Plan: Amazon Web Services AWS 117

2.3 Requirements Management Plan: Amazon Web Services AWS   119

2.4 Requirements Documentation: Amazon Web Services AWS   121

2.5 Requirements Traceability Matrix: Amazon Web Services AWS   123

2.6 Project Scope Statement: Amazon Web Services AWS 125

2.7 Assumption and Constraint Log: Amazon Web Services AWS   127

2.8 Work Breakdown Structure: Amazon Web Services AWS
129

2.9 WBS Dictionary: Amazon Web Services AWS   131

2.10 Schedule Management Plan: Amazon Web Services AWS   133

2.11 Activity List: Amazon Web Services AWS   135

2.12 Activity Attributes: Amazon Web Services AWS   137

2.13 Milestone List: Amazon Web Services AWS   139

2.14 Network Diagram: Amazon Web Services AWS	141

2.15 Activity Resource Requirements: Amazon Web Services AWS	143

2.16 Resource Breakdown Structure: Amazon Web Services AWS	145

2.17 Activity Duration Estimates: Amazon Web Services AWS	147

2.18 Duration Estimating Worksheet: Amazon Web Services AWS	150

2.19 Project Schedule: Amazon Web Services AWS	152

2.20 Cost Management Plan: Amazon Web Services AWS 154

2.21 Activity Cost Estimates: Amazon Web Services AWS 156

2.22 Cost Estimating Worksheet: Amazon Web Services AWS	158

2.23 Cost Baseline: Amazon Web Services AWS	160

2.24 Quality Management Plan: Amazon Web Services AWS	162

2.25 Quality Metrics: Amazon Web Services AWS	164

2.26 Process Improvement Plan: Amazon Web Services AWS	166

2.27 Responsibility Assignment Matrix: Amazon Web Services AWS	168

2.28 Roles and Responsibilities: Amazon Web Services AWS	170

2.29 Human Resource Management Plan: Amazon Web Services AWS 172

2.30 Communications Management Plan: Amazon Web Services AWS 174

2.31 Risk Management Plan: Amazon Web Services AWS 176

2.32 Risk Register: Amazon Web Services AWS 178

2.33 Probability and Impact Assessment: Amazon Web Services AWS 180

2.34 Probability and Impact Matrix: Amazon Web Services AWS 182

2.35 Risk Data Sheet: Amazon Web Services AWS 184

2.36 Procurement Management Plan: Amazon Web Services AWS 186

2.37 Source Selection Criteria: Amazon Web Services AWS 188

2.38 Stakeholder Management Plan: Amazon Web Services AWS 190

2.39 Change Management Plan: Amazon Web Services AWS 192

3.0 Executing Process Group: Amazon Web Services AWS 194

3.1 Team Member Status Report: Amazon Web Services AWS 196

3.2 Change Request: Amazon Web Services AWS 198

3.3 Change Log: Amazon Web Services AWS 200

3.4 Decision Log: Amazon Web Services AWS 202

3.5 Quality Audit: Amazon Web Services AWS 204

3.6 Team Directory: Amazon Web Services AWS 207

3.7 Team Operating Agreement: Amazon Web Services AWS 209

3.8 Team Performance Assessment: Amazon Web Services AWS 211

3.9 Team Member Performance Assessment: Amazon Web Services AWS 213

3.10 Issue Log: Amazon Web Services AWS 215

4.0 Monitoring and Controlling Process Group: Amazon Web Services AWS 217

4.1 Project Performance Report: Amazon Web Services AWS 219

4.2 Variance Analysis: Amazon Web Services AWS 221

4.3 Earned Value Status: Amazon Web Services AWS 223

4.4 Risk Audit: Amazon Web Services AWS 225

4.5 Contractor Status Report: Amazon Web Services AWS 227

4.6 Formal Acceptance: Amazon Web Services AWS 229

5.0 Closing Process Group: Amazon Web Services AWS 231

5.1 Procurement Audit: Amazon Web Services AWS 233

5.2 Contract Close-Out: Amazon Web Services AWS 235

5.3 Project or Phase Close-Out: Amazon Web Services AWS
237

5.4 Lessons Learned: Amazon Web Services AWS   239
Index   242

About The Art of Service

The Art of Service, Business Process Architects since 2000, is dedicated to helping stakeholders achieve excellence.

Defining, designing, creating, and implementing a process to solve a stakeholders challenge or meet an objective is the most valuable role… In EVERY group, company, organization and department.

Unless you're talking a one-time, single-use project, there should be a process. Whether that process is managed and implemented by humans, AI, or a combination of the two, it needs to be designed by someone with a complex enough perspective to ask the right questions.

Someone capable of asking the right questions and step back and say, 'What are we really trying to accomplish here? And is there a different way to look at it?'

With The Art of Service's Standard Requirements Self-Assessments, we empower people who can do just that — whether their title is marketer, entrepreneur, manager, salesperson, consultant, Business Process Manager, executive assistant, IT Manager, CIO etc... —they are the people who rule the future. They are people who watch the process as it happens, and ask the right questions to make the process work better.

Contact us when you need any support with this Self-Assessment and any help with templates, blue-prints and examples of standard documents you might need:

http://theartofservice.com
service@theartofservice.com

Acknowledgments

This checklist was developed under the auspices of The Art of Service, chaired by Gerardus Blokdyk.

Representatives from several client companies participated in the preparation of this Self-Assessment.

Our deepest gratitude goes out to Matt Champagne, Ph.D. Surveys Expert, for his invaluable help and advise in structuring the Self Assessment.

In addition, we are thankful for the design and printing services provided.

Included Resources - how to access

Included with your purchase of the book is the Amazon Web Services AWS Self-Assessment Spreadsheet Dashboard which contains all questions and Self-Assessment areas and auto-generates insights, graphs, and project RACI planning - all with examples to get you started right away.

How? Simply send an email to
access@theartofservice.com
with this books' title in the subject to get the Amazon Web Services AWS Self Assessment Tool right away.

You will receive the following contents with New and Updated specific criteria:
- The latest quick edition of the book in PDF
- The latest complete edition of the book in PDF, which criteria correspond to the criteria in...
- The Self-Assessment Excel Dashboard, and...
- Example pre-filled Self-Assessment Excel Dashboard to get familiar with results generation
- …plus an extra, special, resource that helps you with project managing.

INCLUDES LIFETIME SELF ASSESSMENT UPDATES

Every self assessment comes with Lifetime Updates and Lifetime Free Updated Books. Lifetime Updates is an industry-first feature which allows you to receive verified self assessment updates, ensuring you always have the most accurate information at your fingertips.

Get it now- you will be glad you did - do it now, before you forget.

Send an email to **access@theartofservice.com** with this books' title in the subject to get the Amazon Web Services AWS Self Assessment Tool right away.

Your feedback is invaluable to us

If you recently bought this book, we would love to hear from you! You can do this by writing a review on amazon (or the online store where you purchased this book) about your last purchase! As part of our continual service improvement process, we love to hear real client experiences and feedback.

How does it work?
To post a review on Amazon, just log in to your account and click on the Create Your Own Review button (under Customer Reviews) of the relevant product page. You can find examples of product reviews in Amazon. If you purchased from another online store, simply follow their procedures.

What happens when I submit my review?
Once you have submitted your review, send us an email at review@theartofservice.com with the link to your review so we can properly thank you for your feedback.

Purpose of this Self-Assessment

This Self-Assessment has been developed to improve understanding of the requirements and elements of Amazon Web Services AWS, based on best practices and standards in business process architecture, design and quality management.

It is designed to allow for a rapid Self-Assessment to determine how closely existing management practices and procedures correspond to the elements of the Self-Assessment.

The criteria of requirements and elements of Amazon Web Services AWS have been rephrased in the format of a Self-Assessment questionnaire, with a seven-criterion scoring system, as explained in this document.

In this format, even with limited background knowledge of

Amazon Web Services AWS, a manager can quickly review existing operations to determine how they measure up to the standards. This in turn can serve as the starting point of a 'gap analysis' to identify management tools or system elements that might usefully be implemented in the organization to help improve overall performance.

How to use the Self-Assessment

On the following pages are a series of questions to identify to what extent your Amazon Web Services AWS initiative is complete in comparison to the requirements set in standards.

To facilitate answering the questions, there is a space in front of each question to enter a score on a scale of '1' to '5'.

1 Strongly Disagree

2 Disagree

3 Neutral

4 Agree

5 Strongly Agree

Read the question and rate it with the following in front of mind:

**'In my belief,
the answer to this question is clearly defined'.**

There are two ways in which you can choose to interpret this statement;
1. how aware are you that the answer to the question is clearly defined
2. for more in-depth analysis you can choose to gather

evidence and confirm the answer to the question. This obviously will take more time, most Self-Assessment users opt for the first way to interpret the question and dig deeper later on based on the outcome of the overall Self-Assessment.

A score of '1' would mean that the answer is not clear at all, where a '5' would mean the answer is crystal clear and defined. Leave emtpy when the question is not applicable or you don't want to answer it, you can skip it without affecting your score. Write your score in the space provided.

After you have responded to all the appropriate statements in each section, compute your average score for that section, using the formula provided, and round to the nearest tenth. Then transfer to the corresponding spoke in the Amazon Web Services AWS Scorecard on the second next page of the Self-Assessment.

Your completed Amazon Web Services AWS Scorecard will give you a clear presentation of which Amazon Web Services AWS areas need attention.

Amazon Web Services AWS Scorecard Example

Example of how the finalized Scorecard can look like:

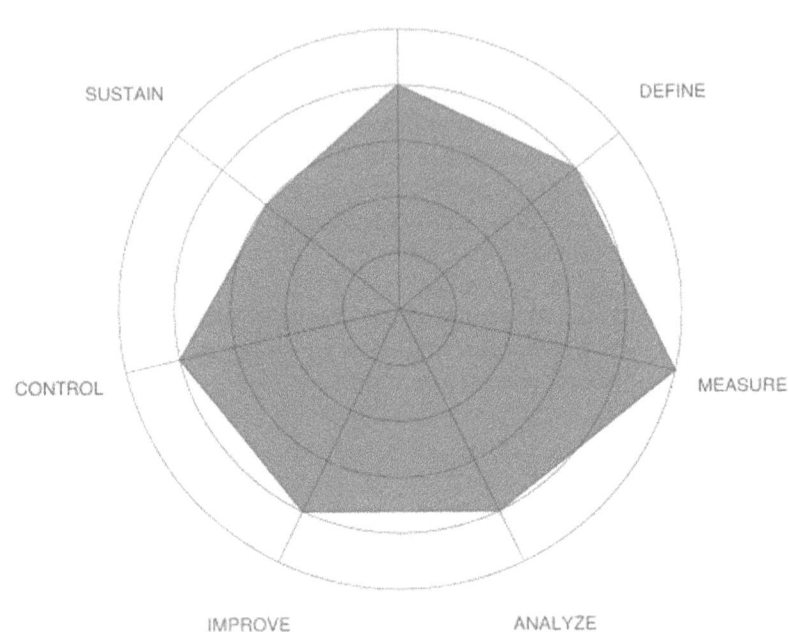

Amazon Web Services AWS Scorecard

Your Scores:

BEGINNING OF THE SELF-ASSESSMENT:

CRITERION #1: RECOGNIZE

INTENT: Be aware of the need for change. Recognize that there is an unfavorable variation, problem or symptom.

In my belief, the answer to this question is clearly defined:

5 Strongly Agree

4 Agree

3 Neutral

2 Disagree

1 Strongly Disagree

1. Are there Amazon Web Services AWS problems defined?
<--- Score

2. How do you identify the kinds of information that you will need?
<--- Score

3. When a Amazon Web Services AWS manager recognizes a problem, what options are available?

<--- Score

4. Can Management personnel recognize the monetary benefit of Amazon Web Services AWS?
<--- Score

5. As a sponsor, customer or management, how important is it to meet goals, objectives?
<--- Score

6. How much are sponsors, customers, partners, stakeholders involved in Amazon Web Services AWS? In other words, what are the risks, if Amazon Web Services AWS does not deliver successfully?
<--- Score

7. How are you going to measure success?
<--- Score

8. What are the business objectives to be achieved with Amazon Web Services AWS?
<--- Score

9. Does Amazon Web Services AWS create potential expectations in other areas that need to be recognized and considered?
<--- Score

10. What situation(s) led to this Amazon Web Services AWS Self Assessment?
<--- Score

11. **What information do users need?**
<--- Score

12. What does Amazon Web Services AWS success

mean to the stakeholders?

<--- Score

13. Who defines the rules in relation to any given issue?

<--- Score

14. How can auditing be a preventative security measure?

<--- Score

15. Why do we need to keep records?

<--- Score

16. Are controls defined to recognize and contain problems?

<--- Score

17. Does our organization need more Amazon Web Services AWS education?

<--- Score

18. Will Amazon Web Services AWS deliverables need to be tested and, if so, by whom?

<--- Score

19. For your Amazon Web Services AWS project, identify and describe the business environment. is there more than one layer to the business environment?

<--- Score

20. What prevents me from making the changes I know will make me a more effective Amazon Web Services AWS leader?

<--- Score

21. Will it solve real problems?

<--- Score

22. What are the expected benefits of Amazon Web Services AWS to the business?
<--- Score

23. How are the Amazon Web Services AWS's objectives aligned to the organization's overall business strategy?
<--- Score

24. What vendors make products that address the Amazon Web Services AWS needs?

<--- Score

25. Do we know what we need to know about this topic?

<--- Score

26. Consider your own Amazon Web Services AWS project. what types of organizational problems do you think might be causing or affecting your problem, based on the work done so far?

<--- Score

27. What is the smallest subset of the problem we can usefully solve?

<--- Score

28. Will a response program recognize when a crisis occurs and provide some level of response?
<--- Score

29. Are there recognized Amazon Web Services AWS

problems?
<--- Score

30. What should be considered when identifying available resources, constraints, and deadlines?
<--- Score

31. Will new equipment/products be required to facilitate Amazon Web Services AWS delivery for example is new software needed?
<--- Score

32. What training and capacity building actions are needed to implement proposed reforms?
<--- Score

33. Are there any specific expectations or concerns about the Amazon Web Services AWS team, Amazon Web Services AWS itself?
<--- Score

34. Cloud management for Amazon Web Services AWS do we really need one?
<--- Score

35. How does it fit into our organizational needs and tasks?
<--- Score

36. Who else hopes to benefit from it?
<--- Score

37. How do we Identify specific Amazon Web Services AWS investment and emerging trends?
<--- Score

38. What would happen if Amazon Web Services AWS weren't done?
<--- Score

39. What problems are you facing and how do you consider Amazon Web Services AWS will circumvent those obstacles?
<--- Score

40. How do you assess your Amazon Web Services AWS workforce capability and capacity needs, including skills, competencies, and staffing levels?
<--- Score

41. Think about the people you identified for your Amazon Web Services AWS project and the project responsibilities you would assign to them. what kind of training do you think they would need to perform these responsibilities effectively?
<--- Score

42. Who had the original idea?
<--- Score

43. What do we need to start doing?
<--- Score

44. Who needs to know about Amazon Web Services AWS ?
<--- Score

45. What tools and technologies are needed for a custom Amazon Web Services AWS project?
<--- Score

46. What else needs to be measured?

<--- Score

47. Is it clear when you think of the day ahead of you what activities and tasks you need to complete?
<--- Score

Add up total points for this section:
_____ = Total points for this section

Divided by: _____ (number of statements answered) = _____
Average score for this section

Transfer your score to the Amazon Web Services AWS Index at the beginning of the Self-Assessment.

CRITERION #2: DEFINE:

INTENT: Formulate the business problem. Define the problem, needs and objectives.

In my belief, the answer to this question is clearly defined:

5 Strongly Agree

4 Agree

3 Neutral

2 Disagree

1 Strongly Disagree

1. Is there a Amazon Web Services AWS management charter, including business case, problem and goal statements, scope, milestones, roles and responsibilities, communication plan?
<--- Score

2. Has the Amazon Web Services AWS work been fairly and/or equitably divided and delegated among team members who are qualified and capable to perform

the work? Has everyone contributed?
<--- Score

3. Has anyone else (internal or external to the organization) attempted to solve this problem or a similar one before? If so, what knowledge can be leveraged from these previous efforts?
<--- Score

4. What are the dynamics of the communication plan?
<--- Score

5. What are the compelling business reasons for embarking on Amazon Web Services AWS?
<--- Score

6. How and when will the baselines be defined?
<--- Score

7. Are there any constraints known that bear on the ability to perform Amazon Web Services AWS work? How is the team addressing them?
<--- Score

8. What customer feedback methods were used to solicit their input?
<--- Score

9. How will variation in the actual durations of each activity be dealt with to ensure that the expected Amazon Web Services AWS results are met?
<--- Score

10. Is Amazon Web Services AWS Required?
<--- Score

11. What specifically is the problem? Where does it occur? When does it occur? What is its extent?
<--- Score

12. How is the team tracking and documenting its work?
<--- Score

13. Is there a completed, verified, and validated high-level 'as is' (not 'should be' or 'could be') business process map?
<--- Score

14. Is the improvement team aware of the different versions of a process: what they think it is vs. what it actually is vs. what it should be vs. what it could be?
<--- Score

15. Have all of the relationships been defined properly?
<--- Score

16. Are improvement team members fully trained on Amazon Web Services AWS?
<--- Score

17. Are business processes mapped?
<--- Score

18. Is the scope of Amazon Web Services AWS defined?
<--- Score

19. Who are the Amazon Web Services AWS improvement team members, including Management Leads and Coaches?

<--- Score

20. Is it clearly defined in and to your organization what you do?
<--- Score

21. How was the 'as is' process map developed, reviewed, verified and validated?
<--- Score

22. What defines Best in Class?
<--- Score

23. What are the boundaries of the scope? What is in bounds and what is not? What is the start point? What is the stop point?
<--- Score

24. Are audit criteria, scope, frequency and methods defined?
<--- Score

25. If substitutes have been appointed, have they been briefed on the Amazon Web Services AWS goals and received regular communications as to the progress to date?
<--- Score

26. What is the minimum educational requirement for potential new hires?
<--- Score

27. Will team members perform Amazon Web Services AWS work when assigned and in a timely fashion?
<--- Score

28. Have all basic functions of Amazon Web Services AWS been defined?
<--- Score

29. Is there regularly 100% attendance at the team meetings? If not, have appointed substitutes attended to preserve cross-functionality and full representation?
<--- Score

30. Is the team equipped with available and reliable resources?
<--- Score

31. Are approval levels defined for contracts and supplements to contracts?
<--- Score

32. How would you define the culture here?
<--- Score

33. When are meeting minutes sent out? Who is on the distribution list?
<--- Score

34. How did the Amazon Web Services AWS manager receive input to the development of a Amazon Web Services AWS improvement plan and the estimated completion dates/times of each activity?
<--- Score

35. Are roles and responsibilities formally defined?
<--- Score

36. Are customers identified and high impact areas defined?

<--- Score

37. Are team charters developed?
<--- Score

38. Is the team formed and are team leaders (Coaches and Management Leads) assigned?
<--- Score

39. Is the team sponsored by a champion or business leader?
<--- Score

40. Have specific policy objectives been defined?
<--- Score

41. How can the value of Amazon Web Services AWS be defined?
<--- Score

42. Has a team charter been developed and communicated?
<--- Score

43. Is the Amazon Web Services AWS scope manageable?
<--- Score

44. Are task requirements clearly defined?
<--- Score

45. What key business process output measure(s) does Amazon Web Services AWS leverage and how?
<--- Score

46. What are the Roles and Responsibilities for each

team member and its leadership? Where is this documented?
<--- Score

47. Is Amazon Web Services AWS linked to key business goals and objectives?
<--- Score

48. Will team members regularly document their Amazon Web Services AWS work?
<--- Score

49. Is Amazon Web Services AWS currently on schedule according to the plan?
<--- Score

50. Is there a critical path to deliver Amazon Web Services AWS results?
<--- Score

51. Has the direction changed at all during the course of Amazon Web Services AWS? If so, when did it change and why?
<--- Score

52. In what way can we redefine the criteria of choice in our category in our favor, as Method introduced style and design to cleaning and Virgin America returned glamor to flying?
<--- Score

53. Who defines (or who defined) the rules and roles?
<--- Score

54. How will the Amazon Web Services AWS team and the organization measure complete success of

Amazon Web Services AWS?
<--- Score

55. Are there different segments of customers?
<--- Score

56. Are Required Metrics Defined?
<--- Score

57. Are different versions of process maps needed to account for the different types of inputs?
<--- Score

58. Do we all define Amazon Web Services AWS in the same way?
<--- Score

59. Are customer(s) identified and segmented according to their different needs and requirements?
<--- Score

60. Has/have the customer(s) been identified?
<--- Score

61. Do the problem and goal statements meet the SMART criteria (specific, measurable, attainable, relevant, and time-bound)?
<--- Score

62. Has a project plan, Gantt chart, or similar been developed/completed?
<--- Score

63. Has everyone on the team, including the team leaders, been properly trained?
<--- Score

64. Is the current 'as is' process being followed? If not, what are the discrepancies?
<--- Score

65. What constraints exist that might impact the team?
<--- Score

66. Are accountability and ownership for Amazon Web Services AWS clearly defined?
<--- Score

67. Is full participation by members in regularly held team meetings guaranteed?
<--- Score

68. How often are the team meetings?
<--- Score

69. How does the Amazon Web Services AWS manager ensure against scope creep?
<--- Score

70. What critical content must be communicated – who, what, when, where, and how?
<--- Score

71. What would be the goal or target for a Amazon Web Services AWS's improvement team?
<--- Score

72. Is there a completed SIPOC representation, describing the Suppliers, Inputs, Process, Outputs, and Customers?
<--- Score

73. When is the estimated completion date?
<--- Score

74. Has a high-level 'as is' process map been completed, verified and validated?
<--- Score

75. How do you keep key subject matter experts in the loop?
<--- Score

76. Does the team have regular meetings?
<--- Score

77. How would one define Amazon Web Services AWS leadership?
<--- Score

78. In what way can we redefine the criteria of choice clients have in our category in our favor?
<--- Score

79. Is data collected and displayed to better understand customer(s) critical needs and requirements.
<--- Score

80. When was the Amazon Web Services AWS start date?
<--- Score

81. Is a fully trained team formed, supported, and committed to work on the Amazon Web Services AWS improvements?
<--- Score

82. What are the rough order estimates on cost savings/opportunities that Amazon Web Services AWS brings?
<--- Score

83. What baselines are required to be defined and managed?
<--- Score

84. Have the customer needs been translated into specific, measurable requirements? How?
<--- Score

85. Has the improvement team collected the 'voice of the customer' (obtained feedback – qualitative and quantitative)?
<--- Score

86. Is the team adequately staffed with the desired cross-functionality? If not, what additional resources are available to the team?
<--- Score

Add up total points for this section:
_____ = Total points for this section

Divided by: _____ (number of statements answered) = _____
Average score for this section

Transfer your score to the Amazon Web Services AWS Index at the beginning of the Self-Assessment.

CRITERION #3: MEASURE:

INTENT: Gather the correct data. Measure the current performance and evolution of the situation.

In my belief, the answer to this question is clearly defined:

5 Strongly Agree

4 Agree

3 Neutral

2 Disagree

1 Strongly Disagree

1. How are you going to measure success?
<--- Score

2. Have all non-recommended alternatives been analyzed in sufficient detail?
<--- Score

3. Is it possible to estimate the impact of unanticipated complexity such as wrong or failed

assumptions, feedback, etc. on proposed reforms?
<--- Score

4. Is Process Variation Displayed/Communicated?
<--- Score

5. What will be measured?
<--- Score

6. How will success or failure be measured?
<--- Score

7. Is a solid data collection plan established that includes measurement systems analysis?
<--- Score

8. When is Knowledge Management Measured?
<--- Score

9. How can you measure Amazon Web Services AWS in a systematic way?
<--- Score

10. How do we focus on what is right -not who is right?
<--- Score

11. Are the measurements objective?
<--- Score

12. Have the types of risks that may impact Amazon Web Services AWS been identified and analyzed?
<--- Score

13. Are process variation components displayed/communicated using suitable charts, graphs, plots?

<--- Score

14. Is long term and short term variability accounted for?
<--- Score

15. Was a data collection plan established?
<--- Score

16. How will your organization measure success?
<--- Score

17. Is performance measured?
<--- Score

18. What measurements are possible, practicable and meaningful?
<--- Score

19. Why identify and analyze stakeholders and their interests?
<--- Score

20. How will you measure your Amazon Web Services AWS effectiveness?
<--- Score

21. What potential environmental factors impact the Amazon Web Services AWS effort?
<--- Score

22. Why should we expend time and effort to implement measurement?
<--- Score

23. Will Amazon Web Services AWS have an impact

on current business continuity, disaster recovery processes and/or infrastructure?
<--- Score

24. What Relevant Entities could be measured?
<--- Score

25. Are there any easy-to-implement alternatives to Amazon Web Services AWS? Sometimes other solutions are available that do not require the cost implications of a full-blown project?
<--- Score

26. Among the Amazon Web Services AWS product and service cost to be estimated, which is considered hardest to estimate?
<--- Score

27. What particular quality tools did the team find helpful in establishing measurements?
<--- Score

28. Schedule Development, Feasibility Analysis, Amazon Web Services AWS Management, Project Closings, Technique: Using the Critical Path Method
<--- Score

29. Have changes been properly/adequately analyzed for effect?
<--- Score

30. Is data collection planned and executed?
<--- Score

31. What is an unallowable cost?
<--- Score

32. What evidence is there and what is measured?
<--- Score

33. Is this an issue for analysis or intuition?
<--- Score

34. How will effects be measured?
<--- Score

35. Which customers cant participate in our Amazon Web Services AWS domain because they lack skills, wealth, or convenient access to existing solutions?
<--- Score

36. Are key measures identified and agreed upon?
<--- Score

37. Can We Measure the Return on Analysis?
<--- Score

38. Does the Amazon Web Services AWS task fit the client's priorities?
<--- Score

39. How do you measure success?
<--- Score

40. What are my customers expectations and measures?
<--- Score

41. Who participated in the data collection for measurements?
<--- Score

42. How will measures be used to manage and adapt?
<--- Score

43. What measurements are being captured?
<--- Score

44. How are measurements made?
<--- Score

45. Meeting the challenge: are missed Amazon Web Services AWS opportunities costing us money?
<--- Score

46. What are the costs of reform?
<--- Score

47. Why do measure/indicators matter?
<--- Score

48. How Will We Measure Success?
<--- Score

49. Why do the measurements/indicators matter?
<--- Score

50. What are measures?
<--- Score

51. How is Knowledge Management Measured?
<--- Score

52. Does Amazon Web Services AWS analysis show the relationships among important Amazon Web Services AWS factors?

<--- Score

53. Do we aggressively reward and promote the people who have the biggest impact on creating excellent Amazon Web Services AWS services/products?
<--- Score

54. Are we taking our company in the direction of better and revenue or cheaper and cost?
<--- Score

55. Which customers can't participate in our market because they lack skills, wealth, or convenient access to existing solutions?
<--- Score

56. What are the agreed upon definitions of the high impact areas, defect(s), unit(s), and opportunities that will figure into the process capability metrics?
<--- Score

57. Do we effectively measure and reward individual and team performance?
<--- Score

58. Does Amazon Web Services AWS analysis isolate the fundamental causes of problems?
<--- Score

59. How do you identify and analyze stakeholders and their interests?
<--- Score

60. Why Measure?
<--- Score

61. What are the key input variables? What are the key process variables? What are the key output variables?
<--- Score

62. What are the uncertainties surrounding estimates of impact?
<--- Score

63. Is key measure data collection planned and executed, process variation displayed and communicated and performance baselined?
<--- Score

64. Can we do Amazon Web Services AWS without complex (expensive) analysis?
<--- Score

65. Is the solution cost-effective?
<--- Score

66. Does the practice systematically track and analyze outcomes related for accountability and quality improvement?
<--- Score

67. How is progress measured?
<--- Score

68. What charts has the team used to display the components of variation in the process?
<--- Score

69. Is there a Performance Baseline?
<--- Score

70. How do we do risk analysis of rare, cascading, catastrophic events?

<--- Score

71. What is the right balance of time and resources between investigation, analysis, and discussion and dissemination?

<--- Score

72. What is measured?

<--- Score

73. What has the team done to assure the stability and accuracy of the measurement process?

<--- Score

74. How to measure variability?

<--- Score

75. Have you found any 'ground fruit' or 'low-hanging fruit' for immediate remedies to the gap in performance?

<--- Score

76. Does Amazon Web Services AWS systematically track and analyze outcomes for accountability and quality improvement?

<--- Score

77. Have the concerns of stakeholders to help identify and define potential barriers been obtained and analyzed?

<--- Score

78. Will We Aggregate Measures across Priorities?

<--- Score

79. Is data collected on key measures that were identified?
<--- Score

80. Are there measurements based on task performance?
<--- Score

81. The approach of traditional Amazon Web Services AWS works for detail complexity but is focused on a systematic approach rather than an understanding of the nature of systems themselves. what approach will permit us to deal with the kind of unpredictable emergent behaviors that dynamic complexity can introduce?
<--- Score

82. What about Amazon Web Services AWS Analysis of results?
<--- Score

83. What should be measured?
<--- Score

84. Are the units of measure consistent?
<--- Score

85. Do staff have the necessary skills to collect, analyze, and report data?
<--- Score

86. What is the total cost related to deploying Amazon Web Services AWS, including any consulting or professional services?
<--- Score

87. Customer Measures: How Do Customers See Us?
<--- Score

88. Where is it measured?
<--- Score

89. What to measure and why?
<--- Score

90. What data was collected (past, present, future/ongoing)?
<--- Score

91. Are losses documented, analyzed, and remedial processes developed to prevent future losses?
<--- Score

92. Which Stakeholder Characteristics Are Analyzed?
<--- Score

93. How do your measurements capture actionable Amazon Web Services AWS information for use in exceeding your customers expectations and securing your customers engagement?
<--- Score

94. How frequently do we track measures?
<--- Score

95. How can we measure the performance?
<--- Score

96. How to measure lifecycle phases?
<--- Score

97. What methods are feasible and acceptable to estimate the impact of reforms?
<--- Score

98. How frequently do you track Amazon Web Services AWS measures?
<--- Score

99. What are your key Amazon Web Services AWS organizational performance measures, including key short and longer-term financial measures?
<--- Score

100. Who should receive measurement reports ?
<--- Score

101. Are you taking your company in the direction of better and revenue or cheaper and cost?
<--- Score

102. How is the value delivered by Amazon Web Services AWS being measured?
<--- Score

103. How large is the gap between current performance and the customer-specified (goal) performance?
<--- Score

104. What key measures identified indicate the performance of the business process?
<--- Score

105. What are our key indicators that you will measure, analyze and track?
<--- Score

106. Are high impact defects defined and identified in the business process?
<--- Score

107. What are the types and number of measures to use?
<--- Score

Add up total points for this section:
_____ = Total points for this section

Divided by: _____ (number of statements answered) = _____
Average score for this section

Transfer your score to the Amazon Web Services AWS Index at the beginning of the Self-Assessment.

CRITERION #4: ANALYZE:

INTENT: Analyze causes, assumptions and hypotheses.

In my belief, the answer to this question is clearly defined:

5 Strongly Agree

4 Agree

3 Neutral

2 Disagree

1 Strongly Disagree

1. What are the revised rough estimates of the financial savings/opportunity for Amazon Web Services AWS improvements?
<--- Score

2. What are the disruptive Amazon Web Services AWS technologies that enable our organization to radically change our business processes?
<--- Score

3. Where is the data coming from to measure compliance?
<--- Score

4. Were there any improvement opportunities identified from the process analysis?
<--- Score

5. Were any designed experiments used to generate additional insight into the data analysis?
<--- Score

6. What quality tools were used to get through the analyze phase?
<--- Score

7. How often will data be collected for measures?
<--- Score

8. What process should we select for improvement?
<--- Score

9. Think about some of the processes you undertake within your organization. which do you own?
<--- Score

10. Did any value-added analysis or 'lean thinking' take place to identify some of the gaps shown on the 'as is' process map?
<--- Score

11. An organizationally feasible system request is one that considers the mission, goals and objectives of the organization. key questions are: is the solution request practical and will it solve a

problem or take advantage of an opportunity to achieve company goals?
<--- Score

12. What conclusions were drawn from the team's data collection and analysis? How did the team reach these conclusions?
<--- Score

13. **How do you measure the Operational performance of your key work systems and processes, including productivity, cycle time, and other appropriate measures of process effectiveness, efficiency, and innovation?**
<--- Score

14. Do you, as a leader, bounce back quickly from setbacks?
<--- Score

15. Is the gap/opportunity displayed and communicated in financial terms?
<--- Score

16. What tools were used to generate the list of possible causes?
<--- Score

17. Were Pareto charts (or similar) used to portray the 'heavy hitters' (or key sources of variation)?
<--- Score

18. **How do you use Amazon Web Services AWS data and information to support organizational decision making and innovation?**
<--- Score

19. Have the problem and goal statements been updated to reflect the additional knowledge gained from the analyze phase?
<--- Score

20. Can we add value to the current Amazon Web Services AWS decision-making process (largely qualitative) by incorporating uncertainty modeling (more quantitative)?
<--- Score

21. Teaches and consults on quality process improvement, project management, and accelerated Amazon Web Services AWS techniques
<--- Score

22. How do we promote understanding that opportunity for improvement is not criticism of the status quo, or the people who created the status quo?
<--- Score

23. What is the cost of poor quality as supported by the team's analysis?
<--- Score

24. What are your current levels and trends in key Amazon Web Services AWS measures or indicators of product and process performance that are important to and directly serve your customers?
<--- Score

25. Identify an operational issue in your organization. for example, could a particular task be done more quickly or more efficiently?

<--- Score

26. What are the best opportunities for value improvement?
<--- Score

27. Is Data and process analysis, root cause analysis and quantifying the gap/opportunity in place?
<--- Score

28. Was a detailed process map created to amplify critical steps of the 'as is' business process?
<--- Score

29. When conducting a business process reengineering study, what should we look for when trying to identify business processes to change?
<--- Score

30. Is the performance gap determined?
<--- Score

31. Did any additional data need to be collected?
<--- Score

32. How is the way you as the leader think and process information affecting your organizational culture?
<--- Score

33. What successful thing are we doing today that may be blinding us to new growth opportunities?
<--- Score

34. What other organizational variables, such as reward systems or communication systems, affect

the performance of this Amazon Web Services AWS process?

<--- Score

35. What were the financial benefits resulting from any 'ground fruit or low-hanging fruit' (quick fixes)?

<--- Score

36. Think about the functions involved in your Amazon Web Services AWS project. what processes flow from these functions?

<--- Score

37. A compounding model resolution with available relevant data can often provide insight towards a solution methodology; which Amazon Web Services AWS models, tools and techniques are necessary?

<--- Score

38. What were the crucial 'moments of truth' on the process map?

<--- Score

39. Do our leaders quickly bounce back from setbacks?

<--- Score

40. How does the organization define, manage, and improve its Amazon Web Services AWS processes?

<--- Score

41. Is the suppliers process defined and controlled?

<--- Score

42. Do your employees have the opportunity to do

what they do best everyday?
<--- Score

43. Have any additional benefits been identified that will result from closing all or most of the gaps?
<--- Score

44. Was a cause-and-effect diagram used to explore the different types of causes (or sources of variation)?
<--- Score

45. Record-keeping requirements flow from the records needed as inputs, outputs, controls and for transformation of a Amazon Web Services AWS process. ask yourself: are the records needed as inputs to the Amazon Web Services AWS process available?
<--- Score

46. Are gaps between current performance and the goal performance identified?
<--- Score

47. What other jobs or tasks affect the performance of the steps in the Amazon Web Services AWS process?
<--- Score

48. What tools were used to narrow the list of possible causes?
<--- Score

49. What does the data say about the performance of the business process?
<--- Score

50. Is the suppliers process defined and controlled?

<--- Score

51. What controls do we have in place to protect data?

<--- Score

52. How do mission and objectives affect the Amazon Web Services AWS processes of our organization?

<--- Score

53. What are our Amazon Web Services AWS Processes?

<--- Score

54. What are your current levels and trends in key measures or indicators of Amazon Web Services AWS product and process performance that are important to and directly serve your customers? how do these results compare with the performance of your competitors and other organizations with similar offerings?

<--- Score

55. What did the team gain from developing a sub-process map?

<--- Score

56. Is the Amazon Web Services AWS process severely broken such that a re-design is necessary?

<--- Score

57. How was the detailed process map generated, verified, and validated?

<--- Score

Add up total points for this section:
_____ = Total points for this section

Divided by: _____ (number of statements answered) = _____
Average score for this section

Transfer your score to the Amazon Web Services AWS Index at the beginning of the Self-Assessment.

CRITERION #5: IMPROVE:

INTENT: Develop a practical solution. Innovate, establish and test the solution and to measure the results.

In my belief, the answer to this question is clearly defined:

5 Strongly Agree

4 Agree

3 Neutral

2 Disagree

1 Strongly Disagree

1. How do we keep improving Amazon Web Services AWS?
<--- Score

2. Are the best solutions selected?
<--- Score

3. What tools were most useful during the improve phase?

<--- Score

4. How will you measure the results?
<--- Score

5. Does the goal represent a desired result that can be measured?
<--- Score

6. What actually has to improve and by how much?
<--- Score

7. How do you manage and improve your Amazon Web Services AWS work systems to deliver customer value and achieve organizational success and sustainability?
<--- Score

8. What attendant changes will need to be made to ensure that the solution is successful?
<--- Score

9. What error proofing will be done to address some of the discrepancies observed in the 'as is' process?
<--- Score

10. Who controls the risk?
<--- Score

11. Are we using Amazon Web Services AWS to communicate information about our Cybersecurity Risk Management programs including the effectiveness of those programs to stakeholders, including boards, investors, auditors, and insurers?
<--- Score

12. How do we decide how much to remunerate an employee?
<--- Score

13. How significant is the improvement in the eyes of the end user?
<--- Score

14. What went well, what should change, what can improve?
<--- Score

15. What to do with the results or outcomes of measurements?
<--- Score

16. How can we improve performance?
<--- Score

17. How does the team improve its work?
<--- Score

18. What tools do you use once you have decided on a Amazon Web Services AWS strategy and more importantly how do you choose?
<--- Score

19. How do we go about Comparing Amazon Web Services AWS approaches/solutions?
<--- Score

20. At what point will vulnerability assessments be performed once Amazon Web Services AWS is put into production (e.g., ongoing Risk Management after implementation)?

<--- Score

21. How to Improve?
<--- Score

22. How do we Improve Amazon Web Services AWS service perception, and satisfaction?
<--- Score

23. Why improve in the first place?
<--- Score

24. Risk factors: what are the characteristics of Amazon Web Services AWS that make it risky?
<--- Score

25. Who controls key decisions that will be made?
<--- Score

26. What tools were used to evaluate the potential solutions?
<--- Score

27. Are new and improved process ('should be') maps developed?
<--- Score

28. How important is the completion of a recognized college or graduate-level degree program in the hiring decision?
<--- Score

29. What were the underlying assumptions on the cost-benefit analysis?
<--- Score

30. What can we do to improve?
<--- Score

31. Do we combine technical expertise with business knowledge and Amazon Web Services AWS Key topics include lifecycles, development approaches, requirements and how to make a business case?
<--- Score

32. What does the 'should be' process map/design look like?
<--- Score

33. How can we improve Amazon Web Services AWS?
<--- Score

34. How do we measure improved Amazon Web Services AWS service perception, and satisfaction?
<--- Score

35. In the past few months, what is the smallest change we have made that has had the biggest positive result? What was it about that small change that produced the large return?
<--- Score

36. What communications are necessary to support the implementation of the solution?
<--- Score

37. How will you know when its improved?
<--- Score

38. If you could go back in time five years, what decision would you make differently? What is your best guess as to what decision you're making today

you might regret five years from now?
<--- Score

39. What tools were used to tap into the creativity and encourage 'outside the box' thinking?
<--- Score

40. Were any criteria developed to assist the team in testing and evaluating potential solutions?
<--- Score

41. What are the implications of this decision 10 minutes, 10 months, and 10 years from now?
<--- Score

42. What is the Amazon Web Services AWS sustainability risk?
<--- Score

43. Is the optimal solution selected based on testing and analysis?
<--- Score

44. Is there a high likelihood that any recommendations will achieve their intended results?
<--- Score

45. How will the team or the process owner(s) monitor the implementation plan to see that it is working as intended?
<--- Score

46. What is the risk?
<--- Score

47. Who are the people involved in developing and implementing Amazon Web Services AWS?
<--- Score

48. Do we cover the five essential competencies-Communication, Collaboration,Innovation, Adaptability, and Leadership that improve an organization's ability to leverage the new Amazon Web Services AWS in a volatile global economy?
<--- Score

49. Is there a small-scale pilot for proposed improvement(s)? What conclusions were drawn from the outcomes of a pilot?
<--- Score

50. How does the solution remove the key sources of issues discovered in the analyze phase?
<--- Score

51. Can the solution be designed and implemented within an acceptable time period?
<--- Score

52. Are we Assessing Amazon Web Services AWS and Risk?
<--- Score

53. Is a contingency plan established?
<--- Score

54. Is pilot data collected and analyzed?
<--- Score

55. How did the team generate the list of possible solutions?

<--- Score

56. Who will be responsible for making the decisions to include or exclude requested changes once Amazon Web Services AWS is underway?
<--- Score

57. What do we want to improve?
<--- Score

58. What is the magnitude of the improvements?
<--- Score

59. What is the team's contingency plan for potential problems occurring in implementation?
<--- Score

60. What evaluation strategy is needed and what needs to be done to assure its implementation and use?
<--- Score

61. Is the measure understandable to a variety of people?
<--- Score

62. What resources are required for the improvement effort?
<--- Score

63. Was a pilot designed for the proposed solution(s)?
<--- Score

64. Who will be using the results of the measurement activities?
<--- Score

65. For estimation problems, how do you develop an estimation statement?
<--- Score

66. Are possible solutions generated and tested?
<--- Score

67. Is Supporting Amazon Web Services AWS documentation required?
<--- Score

68. What is Amazon Web Services AWS's impact on utilizing the best solution(s)?
<--- Score

69. What improvements have been achieved?
<--- Score

70. What is the implementation plan?
<--- Score

71. To what extent does management recognize Amazon Web Services AWS as a tool to increase the results?
<--- Score

72. What actually has to improve and by how much?
<--- Score

73. What lessons, if any, from a pilot were incorporated into the design of the full-scale solution?
<--- Score

74. Are improved process ('should be') maps modified

based on pilot data and analysis?
<--- Score

75. How do we improve productivity?
<--- Score

76. Is there a cost/benefit analysis of optimal solution(s)?
<--- Score

77. Explorations of the frontiers of Amazon Web Services AWS will help you build influence, improve Amazon Web Services AWS, optimize decision making, and sustain change
<--- Score

78. How will the organization know that the solution worked?
<--- Score

79. What needs improvement?
<--- Score

80. Is a solution implementation plan established, including schedule/work breakdown structure, resources, risk management plan, cost/budget, and control plan?
<--- Score

81. Is the solution technically practical?
<--- Score

82. How do we measure risk?
<--- Score

83. How do the Amazon Web Services AWS

results compare with the performance of your competitors and other organizations with similar offerings?
<--- Score

84. How do you improve your likelihood of success ?
<--- Score

85. How Do We Link Measurement and Risk?
<--- Score

86. How do you measure progress and evaluate training effectiveness?
<--- Score

87. How will we know that a change is improvement?
<--- Score

88. What should a proof of concept or pilot accomplish?
<--- Score

89. How can skill-level changes improve Amazon Web Services AWS?
<--- Score

90. Are there any constraints (technical, political, cultural, or otherwise) that would inhibit certain solutions?
<--- Score

91. For decision problems, how do you develop a decision statement?
<--- Score

92. How will you know that you have improved?

<--- Score

93. Is the implementation plan designed?
<--- Score

94. Risk events: what are the things that could go wrong?
<--- Score

95. Describe the design of the pilot and what tests were conducted, if any?
<--- Score

96. Who will be responsible for documenting the Amazon Web Services AWS requirements in detail?
<--- Score

Add up total points for this section:
_____ = Total points for this section

Divided by: _____ (number of statements answered) = _____
Average score for this section

Transfer your score to the Amazon Web Services AWS Index at the beginning of the Self-Assessment.

CRITERION #6: CONTROL:

INTENT: Implement the practical solution. Maintain the performance and correct possible complications.

In my belief, the answer to this question is clearly defined:

5 Strongly Agree

4 Agree

3 Neutral

2 Disagree

1 Strongly Disagree

1. How do controls support value?
<--- Score

2. Is there a transfer of ownership and knowledge to process owner and process team tasked with the responsibilities.
<--- Score

3. Are suggested corrective/restorative actions

indicated on the response plan for known causes to problems that might surface?
<--- Score

4. What are the critical parameters to watch?
<--- Score

5. Is there a control plan in place for sustaining improvements (short and long-term)?
<--- Score

6. Were the planned controls working?
<--- Score

7. Against what alternative is success being measured?
<--- Score

8. Will existing staff require re-training, for example, to learn new business processes?
<--- Score

9. Is there a standardized process?
<--- Score

10. Implementation Planning- is a pilot needed to test the changes before a full roll out occurs?
<--- Score

11. Is new knowledge gained imbedded in the response plan?
<--- Score

12. Is there a recommended audit plan for routine surveillance inspections of Amazon Web Services AWS's gains?

<--- Score

13. What quality tools were useful in the control phase?
<--- Score

14. Is reporting being used or needed?
<--- Score

15. What is your theory of human motivation, and how does your compensation plan fit with that view?
<--- Score

16. Have new or revised work instructions resulted?
<--- Score

17. What do we stand for--and what are we against?
<--- Score

18. What is the recommended frequency of auditing?
<--- Score

19. How will new or emerging customer needs/requirements be checked/communicated to orient the process toward meeting the new specifications and continually reducing variation?
<--- Score

20. What is our theory of human motivation, and how does our compensation plan fit with that view?
<--- Score

21. Are controls in place and consistently applied?
<--- Score

22. What other areas of the organization might benefit from the Amazon Web Services AWS team's improvements, knowledge, and learning?
<--- Score

23. Does Amazon Web Services AWS appropriately measure and monitor risk?
<--- Score

24. Are documented procedures clear and easy to follow for the operators?
<--- Score

25. What key inputs and outputs are being measured on an ongoing basis?
<--- Score

26. What are the known security controls?
<--- Score

27. How will the day-to-day responsibilities for monitoring and continual improvement be transferred from the improvement team to the process owner?
<--- Score

28. How can we best use all of our knowledge repositories to enhance learning and sharing?
<--- Score

29. How likely is the current Amazon Web Services AWS plan to come in on schedule or on budget?
<--- Score

30. Where do ideas that reach policy makers and

planners as proposals for Amazon Web Services AWS strengthening and reform actually originate?
<--- Score

31. What are the key elements of your Amazon Web Services AWS performance improvement system, including your evaluation, organizational learning, and innovation processes?
<--- Score

32. Amazon Web Services AWS in management -Strategic planning
<--- Score

33. Does the response plan contain a definite closed loop continual improvement scheme (e.g., plan-do-check-act)?
<--- Score

34. What are we attempting to measure/monitor?
<--- Score

35. Is knowledge gained on process shared and institutionalized?
<--- Score

36. Are pertinent alerts monitored, analyzed and distributed to appropriate personnel?
<--- Score

37. Can Amazon Web Services AWS be learned?
<--- Score

38. Do the Amazon Web Services AWS decisions we make today help people and the planet tomorrow?
<--- Score

39. In the case of a Amazon Web Services AWS project, the criteria for the audit derive from implementation objectives. an audit of a Amazon Web Services AWS project involves assessing whether the recommendations outlined for implementation have been met. Can we track that any Amazon Web Services AWS project is implemented as planned, and is it working?
<--- Score

40. How will the process owner verify improvement in present and future sigma levels, process capabilities?
<--- Score

41. Who will be in control?
<--- Score

42. What should we measure to verify effectiveness gains?
<--- Score

43. What can you control?
<--- Score

44. Does job training on the documented procedures need to be part of the process team's education and training?
<--- Score

45. How might the organization capture best practices and lessons learned so as to leverage improvements across the business?
<--- Score

46. Why is change control necessary?

<--- Score

47. Do you monitor the effectiveness of your Amazon Web Services AWS activities?
<--- Score

48. What are your results for key measures or indicators of the accomplishment of your Amazon Web Services AWS strategy and action plans, including building and strengthening core competencies?
<--- Score

49. What is the control/monitoring plan?
<--- Score

50. Does a troubleshooting guide exist or is it needed?
<--- Score

51. Whats the best design framework for Amazon Web Services AWS organization now that, in a post industrial-age if the top-down, command and control model is no longer relevant?
<--- Score

52. Is a response plan established and deployed?
<--- Score

53. How will report readings be checked to effectively monitor performance?
<--- Score

54. Do the decisions we make today help people and the planet tomorrow?
<--- Score

55. How will the process owner and team be able to hold the gains?
<--- Score

56. Who is the Amazon Web Services AWS process owner?
<--- Score

57. What should the next improvement project be that is related to Amazon Web Services AWS?
<--- Score

58. How do you encourage people to take control and responsibility?
<--- Score

59. Will any special training be provided for results interpretation?
<--- Score

60. Who has control over resources?
<--- Score

61. Are there documented procedures?
<--- Score

62. What other systems, operations, processes, and infrastructures (hiring practices, staffing, training, incentives/rewards, metrics/dashboards/scorecards, etc.) need updates, additions, changes, or deletions in order to facilitate knowledge transfer and improvements?
<--- Score

63. Is there a Amazon Web Services AWS Communication plan covering who needs to get

what information when?
<--- Score

64. How do you select, collect, align, and integrate Amazon Web Services AWS data and information for tracking daily operations and overall organizational performance, including progress relative to strategic objectives and action plans?
<--- Score

65. Are operating procedures consistent?
<--- Score

66. What should we measure to verify efficiency gains?
<--- Score

67. Does the Amazon Web Services AWS performance meet the customer's requirements?
<--- Score

68. How do our controls stack up?
<--- Score

69. Is there a documented and implemented monitoring plan?
<--- Score

70. Strategic planning -Amazon Web Services AWS relations
<--- Score

71. Has the improved process and its steps been standardized?
<--- Score

72. How will input, process, and output variables be checked to detect for sub-optimal conditions?
<--- Score

73. Is there documentation that will support the successful operation of the improvement?
<--- Score

74. Are new process steps, standards, and documentation ingrained into normal operations?
<--- Score

75. Were the planned controls in place?
<--- Score

76. Do we monitor the Amazon Web Services AWS decisions made and fine tune them as they evolve?
<--- Score

77. Who controls critical resources?
<--- Score

78. Is a response plan in place for when the input, process, or output measures indicate an 'out-of-control' condition?
<--- Score

79. Measure, Monitor and Predict Amazon Web Services AWS Activities to Optimize Operations and Profitably, and Enhance Outcomes
<--- Score

Add up total points for this section:
_____ = Total points for this section

Divided by: _____ (number of

statements answered) = _____
Average score for this section

Transfer your score to the Amazon Web Services AWS Index at the beginning of the Self-Assessment.

CRITERION #7: SUSTAIN:

INTENT: Retain the benefits.

In my belief, the answer to this question is clearly defined:

5 Strongly Agree

4 Agree

3 Neutral

2 Disagree

1 Strongly Disagree

1. How do I stay inspired?
<--- Score

2. **How long will it take to change?**
<--- Score

3. **What are the basics of Amazon Web Services AWS fraud?**
<--- Score

4. **Who are the key stakeholders?**
<--- Score

5. What sources do you use to gather information for a Amazon Web Services AWS study?
<--- Score

6. You may have created your customer policies at a time when you lacked resources, technology wasn't up-to-snuff, or low service levels were the industry norm. Have those circumstances changed?
<--- Score

7. What would have to be true for the option on the table to be the best possible choice?
<--- Score

8. Were lessons learned captured and communicated?
<--- Score

9. Who Uses What?
<--- Score

10. What is it like to work for me?
<--- Score

11. Who is On the Team?
<--- Score

12. What kind of crime could a potential new hire have committed that would not only not disqualify him/her from being hired by our organization, but would actually indicate that he/she might be a particularly good fit?
<--- Score

13. What is the range of capabilities?

<--- Score

14. How to deal with Amazon Web Services AWS Changes?
<--- Score

15. To whom do you add value?
<--- Score

16. What are the Key enablers to make this Amazon Web Services AWS move?
<--- Score

17. Which functions and people interact with the supplier and or customer?
<--- Score

18. Do you see more potential in people than they do in themselves?
<--- Score

19. How much contingency will be available in the budget?
<--- Score

20. Why don't our customers like us?
<--- Score

21. Will there be any necessary staff changes (redundancies or new hires)?
<--- Score

22. How do we keep the momentum going?
<--- Score

23. In what ways are Amazon Web Services AWS

vendors and us interacting to ensure safe and effective use?
<--- Score

24. What is the purpose of Amazon Web Services AWS in relation to the mission?
<--- Score

25. How can you negotiate Amazon Web Services AWS successfully with a stubborn boss, an irate client, or a deceitful coworker?
<--- Score

26. Do Amazon Web Services AWS rules make a reasonable demand on a users capabilities?
<--- Score

27. Who will manage the integration of tools?
<--- Score

28. How do we maintain Amazon Web Services AWS's Integrity?
<--- Score

29. Have new benefits been realized?
<--- Score

30. Ask yourself: how would we do this work if we only had one staff member to do it?
<--- Score

31. Are we / should we be Revolutionary or evolutionary?
<--- Score

32. Why are Amazon Web Services AWS skills

important?
<--- Score

33. Design Thinking: Integrating Innovation, Amazon Web Services AWS, and Brand Value
<--- Score

34. Do you have an implicit bias for capital investments over people investments?
<--- Score

35. What is the funding source for this project?
<--- Score

36. Who do we think the world wants us to be?
<--- Score

37. Are we changing as fast as the world around us?
<--- Score

38. What management system can we use to leverage the Amazon Web Services AWS experience, ideas, and concerns of the people closest to the work to be done?
<--- Score

39. What is Effective Amazon Web Services AWS?
<--- Score

40. Who will use it?
<--- Score

41. When information truly is ubiquitous, when reach and connectivity are completely global, when computing resources are infinite, and when a whole new set of impossibilities are not only possible, but

happening, what will that do to our business?
<--- Score

42. What would I recommend my friend do if he were facing this dilemma?
<--- Score

43. Who are four people whose careers I've enhanced?
<--- Score

44. Is maximizing Amazon Web Services AWS protection the same as minimizing Amazon Web Services AWS loss?
<--- Score

45. What are the usability implications of Amazon Web Services AWS actions?
<--- Score

46. If no one would ever find out about my accomplishments, how would I lead differently?
<--- Score

47. Who is going to care?
<--- Score

48. Why should we adopt a Amazon Web Services AWS framework?
<--- Score

49. Are we paying enough attention to the partners our company depends on to succeed?
<--- Score

50. What are we challenging, in the sense that Mac challenged the PC or Dove tackled the Beauty Myth?

<--- Score

51. How are we doing compared to our industry?
<--- Score

52. How do you determine the key elements that affect Amazon Web Services AWS workforce satisfaction? how are these elements determined for different workforce groups and segments?
<--- Score

53. Who is responsible for ensuring appropriate resources (time, people and money) are allocated to Amazon Web Services AWS?
<--- Score

54. What do we do when new problems arise?
<--- Score

55. Do we have the right capabilities and capacities?
<--- Score

56. What happens when a new employee joins the organization?
<--- Score

57. If our customer were my grandmother, would I tell her to buy what we're selling?
<--- Score

58. What is the overall business strategy?
<--- Score

59. What one word do we want to own in the minds of our customers, employees, and partners?

<--- Score

60. How do senior leaders deploy your organizations vision and values through your leadership system, to the workforce, to key suppliers and partners, and to customers and other stakeholders, as appropriate?
<--- Score

61. Operational - will it work?
<--- Score

62. What should we stop doing?
<--- Score

63. What stupid rule would we most like to kill?
<--- Score

64. Am I failing differently each time?
<--- Score

65. Think about the kind of project structure that would be appropriate for your Amazon Web Services AWS project. should it be formal and complex, or can it be less formal and relatively simple?
<--- Score

66. How do we engage the workforce, in addition to satisfying them?
<--- Score

67. What is the mission of the organization?
<--- Score

68. Do we underestimate the customer's journey?

<--- Score

69. Amazon Web Services AWS Service Sales Supply Chain, Procurement, Distribution
<--- Score

70. What happens at this company when people fail?
<--- Score

71. What is our formula for success in Amazon Web Services AWS ?
<--- Score

72. What did we miss in the interview for the worst hire we ever made?
<--- Score

73. Are we making progress? and are we making progress as Amazon Web Services AWS leaders?
<--- Score

74. What are the business goals Amazon Web Services AWS is aiming to achieve?
<--- Score

75. What threat is Amazon Web Services AWS addressing?
<--- Score

76. What are your most important goals for the strategic Amazon Web Services AWS objectives?
<--- Score

77. Do we say no to customers for no reason?
<--- Score

78. What business benefits will Amazon Web Services AWS goals deliver if achieved?
<--- Score

79. How likely is it that a customer would recommend our company to a friend or colleague?
<--- Score

80. If there were zero limitations, what would we do differently?
<--- Score

81. What is Tricky About This?
<--- Score

82. Are the assumptions believable and achievable?
<--- Score

83. Instead of going to current contacts for new ideas, what if you reconnected with dormant contacts-- the people you used to know? If you were going reactivate a dormant tie, who would it be?
<--- Score

84. What are the short and long-term Amazon Web Services AWS goals?
<--- Score

85. What new services of functionality will be implemented next with Amazon Web Services AWS ?
<--- Score

86. Is our strategy driving our strategy? Or is the way in which we allocate resources driving our strategy?

<--- Score

87. Are new benefits received and understood?
<--- Score

88. How Do We Create Buy-in?
<--- Score

89. How important is Amazon Web Services AWS to the user organizations mission?
<--- Score

90. What is the craziest thing we can do?
<--- Score

91. What are the success criteria that will indicate that Amazon Web Services AWS objectives have been met and the benefits delivered?
<--- Score

92. Have benefits been optimized with all key stakeholders?
<--- Score

93. Who, on the executive team or the board, has spoken to a customer recently?
<--- Score

94. How Do We Know if We Are Successful?
<--- Score

95. Can we maintain our growth without detracting from the factors that have contributed to our success?
<--- Score

96. In the past year, what have you done (or could you have done) to increase the accurate perception of this company/brand as ethical and honest?
<--- Score

97. Will it be accepted by users?
<--- Score

98. What is something you believe that nearly no one agrees with you on?
<--- Score

99. Whose voice (department, ethnic group, women, older workers, etc) might you have missed hearing from in your company, and how might you amplify this voice to create positive momentum for your business?
<--- Score

100. Do I know what I'm doing? And who do I call if I don't?
<--- Score

101. Do we think we know, or do we know we know ?
<--- Score

102. Do you keep 50% of your time unscheduled?
<--- Score

103. Who else should we help?
<--- Score

104. Who do we want our customers to become?
<--- Score

105. What are the rules and assumptions my industry operates under? What if the opposite were true?
<--- Score

106. Who have we, as a company, historically been when we've been at our best?
<--- Score

107. Is there a limit on the number of users in Amazon Web Services AWS ?
<--- Score

108. What is your BATNA (best alternative to a negotiated agreement)?
<--- Score

109. If we do not follow, then how to lead?
<--- Score

110. What is our question?
<--- Score

111. Which Amazon Web Services AWS goals are the most important?
<--- Score

112. Which models, tools and techniques are necessary?
<--- Score

113. Who will determine interim and final deadlines?
<--- Score

114. What is an unauthorized commitment?
<--- Score

115. What are all of our Amazon Web Services AWS domains and what do they do?

<--- Score

116. Would you rather sell to knowledgeable and informed customers or to uninformed customers?

<--- Score

117. What happens if you do not have enough funding?

<--- Score

118. What are internal and external Amazon Web Services AWS relations?

<--- Score

119. In retrospect, of the projects that we pulled the plug on, what percent do we wish had been allowed to keep going, and what percent do we wish had ended earlier?

<--- Score

120. Are the criteria for selecting recommendations stated?

<--- Score

121. Who is the main stakeholder, with ultimate responsibility for driving Amazon Web Services AWS forward?

<--- Score

122. What current systems have to be understood and/or changed?

<--- Score

123. How do we foster the skills, knowledge, talents, attributes, and characteristics we want to have?
<--- Score

124. Why should people listen to you?
<--- Score

125. How do we Lead with Amazon Web Services AWS in Mind?
<--- Score

126. How does Amazon Web Services AWS integrate with other business initiatives?
<--- Score

127. How can we become more high-tech but still be high touch?
<--- Score

128. What have we done to protect our business from competitive encroachment?
<--- Score

129. Do you have a vision statement?
<--- Score

130. What counts that we are not counting?
<--- Score

131. How will we ensure we get what we expected?
<--- Score

132. Is there any existing Amazon Web Services AWS governance structure?
<--- Score

133. Which individuals, teams or departments will be involved in Amazon Web Services AWS?
<--- Score

134. Who will provide the final approval of Amazon Web Services AWS deliverables?
<--- Score

135. What knowledge, skills and characteristics mark a good Amazon Web Services AWS project manager?
<--- Score

136. Who will be responsible for deciding whether Amazon Web Services AWS goes ahead or not after the initial investigations?
<--- Score

137. What is a feasible sequencing of reform initiatives over time?
<--- Score

138. What will be the consequences to the stakeholder (financial, reputation etc) if Amazon Web Services AWS does not go ahead or fails to deliver the objectives?
<--- Score

139. Among our stronger employees, how many see themselves at the company in three years? How many would leave for a 10 percent raise from another company?
<--- Score

140. Are assumptions made in Amazon Web

Services AWS stated explicitly?

<--- Score

141. Do you have any supplemental information to add to this checklist?

<--- Score

142. What is the estimated value of the project?

<--- Score

143. What are specific Amazon Web Services AWS Rules to follow?

<--- Score

144. Is it economical; do we have the time and money?

<--- Score

145. We picked a method, now what?

<--- Score

146. Do we have the right people on the bus?

<--- Score

147. Is the Amazon Web Services AWS organization completing tasks effectively and efficiently?

<--- Score

148. How will we build a 100-year startup?

<--- Score

149. Is there any reason to believe the opposite of my current belief?

<--- Score

150. What are the top 3 things at the forefront of

our Amazon Web Services AWS agendas for the next 3 years?

<--- Score

151. How do we go about Securing Amazon Web Services AWS?

<--- Score

152. Whom among your colleagues do you trust, and for what?

<--- Score

153. What trophy do we want on our mantle?

<--- Score

154. Why is it important to have senior management support for a Amazon Web Services AWS project?

<--- Score

155. What information is critical to our organization that our executives are ignoring?

<--- Score

156. Is a Amazon Web Services AWS Team Work effort in place?

<--- Score

157. How to Secure Amazon Web Services AWS?

<--- Score

158. What is our competitive advantage?

<--- Score

159. How do we manage Amazon Web Services AWS Knowledge Management (KM)?

<--- Score

160. If we got kicked out and the board brought in a new CEO, what would he do?
<--- Score

161. What potential megatrends could make our business model obsolete?
<--- Score

162. What are the Essentials of Internal Amazon Web Services AWS Management?
<--- Score

163. What are the gaps in my knowledge and experience?
<--- Score

164. How do we make it meaningful in connecting Amazon Web Services AWS with what users do day-to-day?
<--- Score

165. If you had to rebuild your organization without any traditional competitive advantages (i.e., no killer a technology, promising research, innovative product/service delivery model, etc.), how would your people have to approach their work and collaborate together in order to create the necessary conditions for success?
<--- Score

166. What are strategies for increasing support and reducing opposition?
<--- Score

167. If I had to leave my organization for a year and the only communication I could have with employees was a single paragraph, what would I write?
<--- Score

168. Is Amazon Web Services AWS dependent on the successful delivery of a current project?
<--- Score

169. Who can I speak to in order to receive help about amazon web services aws?
<--- Score

170. Who uses our product in ways we never expected?
<--- Score

171. What are the challenges?
<--- Score

172. What is our Amazon Web Services AWS Strategy?
<--- Score

173. Do we have enough freaky customers in our portfolio pushing us to the limit day in and day out?
<--- Score

174. In a project to restructure Amazon Web Services AWS outcomes, which stakeholders would you involve?
<--- Score

175. Will I get fired?
<--- Score

176. How would our PR, marketing, and social media

change if we did not use outside agencies?
<--- Score

177. Where can we break convention?
<--- Score

178. What am I trying to prove to myself, and how might it be hijacking my life and business success?
<--- Score

179. Who is responsible for errors?
<--- Score

180. If you were responsible for initiating and implementing major changes in your organization, what steps might you take to ensure acceptance of those changes?
<--- Score

181. Who are you going to put out of business, and why?
<--- Score

182. How is business? Why?
<--- Score

183. Which criteria are used to determine which projects are going to be pursued or discarded?
<--- Score

184. How do we foster innovation?
<--- Score

185. Are you satisfied with your current role? If not, what is missing from it?
<--- Score

186. Political -is anyone trying to undermine this project?
<--- Score

187. Are there Amazon Web Services AWS Models?
<--- Score

188. How will you know that the Amazon Web Services AWS project has been successful?
<--- Score

189. If we weren't already in this business, would we enter it today? And if not, what are we going to do about it?
<--- Score

190. How do we accomplish our long range Amazon Web Services AWS goals?
<--- Score

191. What was the last experiment we ran?
<--- Score

192. How much does Amazon Web Services AWS help?
<--- Score

193. Marketing budgets are tighter, consumers are more skeptical, and social media has changed forever the way we talk about Amazon Web Services AWS. How do we gain traction?
<--- Score

194. Schedule -can it be done in the given time?
<--- Score

195. Your reputation and success is your lifeblood, and Amazon Web Services AWS shows you how to stay relevant, add value, and win and retain customers
<--- Score

196. What will drive Amazon Web Services AWS change?
<--- Score

197. What may be the consequences for the performance of an organization if all stakeholders are not consulted regarding Amazon Web Services AWS?
<--- Score

198. If our company went out of business tomorrow, would anyone who doesn't get a paycheck here care?
<--- Score

199. How do we provide a safe environment -physically and emotionally?
<--- Score

200. Is the impact that Amazon Web Services AWS has shown?
<--- Score

201. What trouble can we get into?
<--- Score

202. What are the critical success factors?
<--- Score

203. Where is our petri dish?
<--- Score

204. How do we ensure that implementations of Amazon Web Services AWS products are done in a way that ensures safety?

<--- Score

205. How can we incorporate support to ensure safe and effective use of Amazon Web Services AWS into the services that we provide?

<--- Score

206. Who sets the Amazon Web Services AWS standards?

<--- Score

207. What does your signature ensure?

<--- Score

208. Are we relevant? Will we be relevant five years from now? Ten?

<--- Score

209. Has implementation been effective in reaching specified objectives?

<--- Score

210. Think of your Amazon Web Services AWS project. what are the main functions?

<--- Score

211. How will we know if we have been successful?

<--- Score

212. How can we become the company that would put us out of business?

<--- Score

213. Are there any disadvantages to implementing Amazon Web Services AWS? There might be some that are less obvious?
<--- Score

214. What role does communication play in the success or failure of a Amazon Web Services AWS project?
<--- Score

215. What are the long-term Amazon Web Services AWS goals?
<--- Score

216. How will we insure seamless interoperability of Amazon Web Services AWS moving forward?
<--- Score

217. Design Thinking: Integrating Innovation, Amazon Web Services AWS Experience, and Brand Value
<--- Score

218. Did my employees make progress today?
<--- Score

Add up total points for this section:
_____ = Total points for this section

Divided by: _____ (number of statements answered) = _____
Average score for this section

Transfer your score to the Amazon Web Services AWS Index at the beginning of the Self-Assessment.

Amazon Web Services AWS and Managing Projects, Criteria for Project Managers:

1.0 Initiating Process Group: Amazon Web Services AWS

1. Based on your Amazon Web Services AWS project communication management plan, what worked well?

2. Just how important is your work to the overall success of the Amazon Web Services AWS project?

3. Does it make any difference if I am successful?

4. Are identified risks being monitored properly, are new risks arising during the Amazon Web Services AWS project or are foreseen risks occurring?

5. What areas does the group agree are the biggest success on the Amazon Web Services AWS project?

6. Establishment of PM Office?

7. When will the Amazon Web Services AWS project be done?

8. If action is called for, what form should it take?

9. Who is performing the work of the Amazon Web Services AWS project?

10. Am I just doing busywork to pass the time?

11. Have requirements been tested, approved, and fulfill the Amazon Web Services AWS project scope?

12. When must it be done?

13. Do you know if the Amazon Web Services AWS project requires outside equipment or vendor resources?

14. Do you understand the quality and control criteria that must be achieved for successful Amazon Web Services AWS project completion?

15. How can I make my needs known?

16. Are stakeholders properly informed about the status of the Amazon Web Services AWS project?

17. What will you do to minimize the impact should a risk event occur?

18. What is the NEXT thing to do?

19. Were resources available as planned?

20. What areas were overlooked on this Amazon Web Services AWS project?

1.1 Project Charter: Amazon Web Services AWS

21. Why Do you Manage Integration?

22. What are the known stakeholder requirements?

23. Why use a Amazon Web Services AWS project charter?

24. Who is the Amazon Web Services AWS project Manager?

25. What is the justification?

26. Strategic Fit: What is the Strategic Initiative Identifier for this Amazon Web Services AWS project?

27. How much?

28. What are the assumptions?

29. Will this replace an existing product?

30. Does the Amazon Web Services AWS project need to consider any special capacity or capability issues?

31. What are the deliverables?

32. What changes can you make to improve?

33. Run it as as a startup?

34. Assumptions and Constraints: What assumptions were made in defining Amazon Web Services AWS project?

35. What are the constraints?

36. Assumptions: What factors, for planning purposes, are you considering to be true?

37. How will you know that a change is an improvement?

38. What metrics could you look at?

39. Did your Amazon Web Services AWS project ask for this?

40. Amazon Web Services AWS project Background: What is the primary motivation for this Amazon Web Services AWS project?

1.2 Stakeholder Register: Amazon Web Services AWS

41. How much influence do they have on the Amazon Web Services AWS project?

42. What opportunities exist to provide communications?

43. Who are the stakeholders?

44. How Big is the Gap?

45. What are the major Amazon Web Services AWS project milestones requiring communications or providing communications opportunities?

46. What is the power of the stakeholder?

47. Who is Managing Stakeholder Engagement?

48. How will Reports Be Created?

49. Who wants to talk about Security?

50. How should employers make their voices heard?

51. What & Why?

52. Is Your Organization Ready for Change?

1.3 Stakeholder Analysis Matrix: Amazon Web Services AWS

53. Who determines value?

54. Accreditations, qualifications, certifications?

55. Partnerships, agencies, distribution?

56. Processes, systems, IT, communications?

57. How affected by the problem(s)?

58. Price, value, quality?

59. Sustaining internal capabilities?

60. Economy - home, abroad?

61. What is Accountability in relation to the Amazon Web Services AWS project?

62. What is their relationship with the Amazon Web Services AWS project?

63. Guiding question: What is the issue at stake?

64. Who is directly responsible for decisions on issues important to the Amazon Web Services AWS project?

65. How can you counter negative efforts?

66. What obstacles does the organization face?

67. What can the Amazon Web Services AWS projects outcome be used for?

68. Competitors vulnerabilities?

69. Are they likely to influence the success or failure of your Amazon Web Services AWS project?

70. Effects on core activities, distraction?

71. What's in it for you?

72. Why is it important to identify them?

2.0 Planning Process Group: Amazon Web Services AWS

73. Is the organization showing technical capacity and leadership commitment to keep working with the Amazon Web Services AWS project and to repeat it?

74. How well will the chosen processes produce the expected results?

75. How Will You Know You Did It?

76. To what extent has the intervention strategy been adapted to the areas of intervention in which it is being implemented?

77. Why is it important to determine activity sequencing on Amazon Web Services AWS projects?

78. Is the Amazon Web Services AWS project supported by national and/or local organizations?

79. To what extent have the target population and participants made the activities their own, taking an active role in it?

80. What factors are contributing to progress or delay in the achievement of products and results?

81. On which process should team members spend the most time?

82. First of all, should any action be taken?

83. Are the follow-up indicators relevant and do they meet the quality needed to measure the outputs and outcomes of the Amazon Web Services AWS project?

84. How do you integrate Amazon Web Services AWS project Planning with the Iterative/Evolutionary SDLC?

85. Is the identification of the problems, inequalities and gaps, with their respective causes, clear in the Amazon Web Services AWS project?

86. How many days can task X be late in starting without affecting the Amazon Web Services AWS project completion date?

87. How can you tell when you are done?

88. How are IT Amazon Web Services AWS projects different?

89. Will you be replaced?

90. In what way has the Amazon Web Services AWS project come up with innovative measures for problem-solving?

91. What types of differentiated effects are resulting from the Amazon Web Services AWS project and to what extent?

2.1 Project Management Plan: Amazon Web Services AWS

92. Is the budget realistic?

93. How well are you able to manage your risk?

94. What goes into your Amazon Web Services AWS project Charter?

95. What should you drop in order to add something new?

96. What happened during the process that you found interesting?

97. What Went Wrong?

98. What does management expect of PMs?

99. Does the implementation plan have an appropriate division of responsibilities?

100. Does the selected plan protect privacy?

101. What are the training needs?

102. If the Amazon Web Services AWS project management plan is a comprehensive document that guides you in Amazon Web Services AWS project execution and control, then what should it NOT contain?

103. Will you add a schedule and diagram?

104. How do you manage time?

105. Are cost risk analysis methods applied to develop contingencies for the estimated total Amazon Web Services AWS project costs?

106. What Went Right?

107. Do the proposed changes from the Amazon Web Services AWS project include any significant risks to safety?

108. Has the selected plan been formulated using cost effectiveness and incremental analysis techniques?

109. Are alternatives safe, functional, constructible, economical, reasonable and sustainable?

2.2 Scope Management Plan: Amazon Web Services AWS

110. Does the Business Case include how the Amazon Web Services AWS project aligns with the organizations strategic goals & objectives?

111. Timeline and milestones?

112. Will your organizations estimating methodology be used and followed?

113. Does the detailed Amazon Web Services AWS project plan identify individual responsibilities for the next 4–6 weeks?

114. Are individual tasks of reasonable time effort (8–40 hours)?

115. Is the assigned Amazon Web Services AWS project manager a PMP (Certified Amazon Web Services AWS project manager) and experienced?

116. Has a provision been made to reassess Amazon Web Services AWS project risks at various Amazon Web Services AWS project stages?

117. What are the risks that could significantly affect the resources needed for the Amazon Web Services AWS project?

118. Are the budget estimates reasonable?

119. What are the Quality Assurance overheads?

120. Do you have funding for Amazon Web Services AWS project and product development, implementation and on-going support?

121. Has the Amazon Web Services AWS project manager been identified?

122. Are Vendor contract reports, reviews and visits conducted periodically?

123. Are tasks tracked by hours?

124. Has the scope management document been updated and distributed to help prevent scope creep?

125. When is corrective or preventative action required?

126. Are you doing what you have set out to do?

127. Does a documented Amazon Web Services AWS project organizational policy & plan (i.e. governance model) exist?

128. Are Amazon Web Services AWS project contact logs kept up to date?

129. What happens if scope changes?

2.3 Requirements Management Plan: Amazon Web Services AWS

130. How often will the reporting occur?

131. If it exists, where is it housed?

132. Could inaccurate or incomplete requirements in this Amazon Web Services AWS project create a serious risk for the business?

133. Is infrastructure setup part of your Amazon Web Services AWS project?

134. Should you include sub-activities?

135. Did you avoid subjective, flowery or non-specific statements?

136. Will the Amazon Web Services AWS project requirements become approved in writing?

137. What information regarding the Amazon Web Services AWS project requirements will be reported?

138. How will you communicate scheduled tasks to other team members?

139. Which hardware or software, related to, or as outcome of the Amazon Web Services AWS project is new to the organization?

140. How will unresolved questions be handled once

approval has been obtained?

141. How knowledgeable is the team in the proposed application area?

142. Who will initially review the Amazon Web Services AWS project work or products to ensure it meets the applicable acceptance criteria?

143. Will you perform a Requirements Risk assessment and develop a plan to deal with risks?

144. Who will finally present the work or product(s) for acceptance?

145. Why Manage Requirements?

146. Subject to Change Control?

147. Are actual resource expenditures versus planned still acceptable?

148. What is a problem?

2.4 Requirements Documentation: Amazon Web Services AWS

149. Where do you define what is a customer, what are the attributes of customer?

150. How much testing do you need to do to prove that my system is safe?

151. Do your Constraints stand?

152. What happens when requirements are wrong?

153. Is the requirement properly understood?

154. How can you document system requirements?

155. Have the benefits identified with the system being identified clearly?

156. What if the system wasn t implemented?

157. What are the potential disadvantages/advantages?

158. What is your Elevator Speech?

159. How do you know when a Requirement is accurate enough?

160. What kind of entity is a problem ?

161. Does your company restrict technical

alternatives?

162. Are there any requirements conflicts?

163. Does the system provide the functions which best support the customers needs?

164. What is the risk associated with cost and schedule?

165. Who is interacting with the system?

166. Are there legal issues?

167. What marketing channels do you want to use: e-mail, letter or sms?

168. What are the acceptance criteria?

2.5 Requirements Traceability Matrix: Amazon Web Services AWS

169. Is there a requirements traceability process in place?

170. Why use a WBS?

171. What is the WBS?

172. Describe the process for approving requirements so they can be added to the traceability matrix and Amazon Web Services AWS project work can be performed. Will the Amazon Web Services AWS project requirements become approved in writing?

173. How small is small enough?

174. What percentage of Amazon Web Services AWS projects are producing traceability matrices between requirements and other work products?

175. Why Do you Manage Scope?

176. How Do you Manage Scope?

177. How will it affect the stakeholders personally in their career?

178. Will you use a Requirements Traceability Matrix?

179. Do we have a clear understanding of all subcontracts in place?

180. What are the chronologies, contingencies, consequences, criteria?

2.6 Project Scope Statement: Amazon Web Services AWS

181. Is there an information system for the Amazon Web Services AWS project?

182. What are the defined meeting materials?

183. What are some of the major deliverables of the Amazon Web Services AWS project?

184. Was planning completed before the Amazon Web Services AWS project was initiated?

185. If there is an independent oversight contractor, have they signed off on the Amazon Web Services AWS project Plan?

186. Will all Amazon Web Services AWS project issues be unconditionally tracked through the issue resolution process?

187. Is there a Change Management Board?

188. Have you been able to easily identify success criteria and create objective measurements for each of the Amazon Web Services AWS project scopes goal statements?

189. If you were to write a list of what should not be included in the scope statement, what are some of the things that you would recommend be described as out-of-scope?

190. Will the Amazon Web Services AWS project risks being managed be according to the Amazon Web Services AWS projects risk management process?

191. Once its defined, what is the stability of the Amazon Web Services AWS project scope?

192. Is there a baseline plan against which to measure progress?

193. Has the format for tracking and monitoring schedules and costs been defined?

194. Is the quality function identified and assigned?

195. Is the plan under configuration management?

196. Are there issues that could affect the existing requirements for the result, service, or product if the scope changes?

197. Do you anticipate new stakeholders joining the Amazon Web Services AWS project over time?

198. Have you been able to thoroughly document the Amazon Web Services AWS projects assumptions and constraints?

2.7 Assumption and Constraint Log: Amazon Web Services AWS

199. What Threats might prevent us from getting there?

200. No superfluous information or marketing narrative?

201. Were the system requirements formally reviewed prior to initiating the design phase?

202. Are there unnecessary steps that are creating bottlenecks and/or causing people to wait?

203. Does the system design reflect the requirements?

204. Has a Amazon Web Services AWS project Communications Plan been developed?

205. Is the definition of the Amazon Web Services AWS project scope clear; what needs to be accomplished?

206. What Weaknesses do you have?

207. Have Amazon Web Services AWS project management standards and procedures been established and documented?

208. Does the traceability documentation describe the tool and/or mechanism to be used to capture traceability throughout the life cycle?

209. Is there adequate stakeholder participation for the vetting of requirements definition, changes and management?

210. Do documented requirements exist for all critical components and areas, including technical, business, interfaces, performance, security and conversion requirements?

211. Is there a Steering Committee in place?

212. Have adequate resources been provided by management to ensure Amazon Web Services AWS project success?

213. Diagrams and tables are included to explain complex concepts and increase overall readability?

214. Are there cosmetic errors that hinder readability and comprehension?

215. Does a specific action and/or state that is known to violate security policy occur?

216. What would you gain if you spent time working to improve this process?

217. Can the requirements be traced to the appropriate components of the solution, as well as test scripts?

218. Have all involved stakeholders and work groups committed to the Amazon Web Services AWS project?

2.8 Work Breakdown Structure: Amazon Web Services AWS

219. Where does it take place?

220. How will you and your Amazon Web Services AWS project team define the Amazon Web Services AWS projects scope and work breakdown structure?

221. Do you need another level?

222. When would you develop a Work Breakdown Structure?

223. Why would you develop a Work Breakdown Structure?

224. What has to be done?

225. What is the probability of completing the Amazon Web Services AWS project in less that xx days?

226. Is the Work breakdown Structure (WBS) defined and is the scope of the Amazon Web Services AWS project clear with assigned deliverable owners?

227. Is it a change in scope?

228. Is it still viable?

229. When do you stop?

230. How much detail?

231. What is the probability that the Amazon Web Services AWS project duration will exceed xx weeks?

232. Why is it useful?

233. How big is a work-package?

234. Can you make it?

235. When does it have to be done?

236. How Far Down?

237. How many levels?

238. Who has to do it?

2.9 WBS Dictionary: Amazon Web Services AWS

239. Is the work done on a work package level as described in the WBS dictionary?

240. Are the rates for allocating costs from each indirect cost pool to contracts updated as necessary to ensure a realistic monthly allocation of indirect costs without significant year-end adjustments?

241. Changes in the current direct and Amazon Web Services AWS projected base?

242. Actual cost of work performed?

243. Are time-phased budgets established for planning and control of level of effort activity by category of resource; for example, type of manpower and/or material?

244. Does the cost accumulation system provide for summarization of indirect costs from the point of allocation to the contract total?

245. Evaluate the performance of operating organizations?

246. Detailed schedules which support control account and work package start and completion dates/events?

247. Contemplated overhead expenditure for each

period based on the best information currently available?

248. Does the contractors system include procedures for measuring performance of the lowest level organization responsible for the control account?

249. How detailed should a Amazon Web Services AWS project get?

250. Are retroactive changes to BCWS and BCWP prohibited except for correction of errors or for normal accounting adjustments?

251. Where learning is used in developing underlying budgets is there a direct relationship between anticipated learning and time phased budgets?

252. Are estimates of costs at completion generated in a rational, consistent manner?

253. Incurrence of actual indirect costs in excess of budgets, by element of expense?

254. Are the contractors estimates of costs at completion reconcilable with cost data reported to us?

255. Are procedures established to prevent changes to the contract budget base other than those authorized by contractual action?

256. Are all elements of indirect expense identified to overhead cost budgets of Amazon Web Services AWS projections?

2.10 Schedule Management Plan: Amazon Web Services AWS

257. What s the difference between % Complete and % work?

258. Are all resource assumptions documented?

259. Are Amazon Web Services AWS project leaders committed to this Amazon Web Services AWS project full time?

260. Staffing Requirements?

261. What happens if a warning is triggered?

262. Are scheduled deliverables actually delivered?

263. Cost / Benefit Analysis?

264. Are software metrics formally captured, analyzed and used as a basis for other Amazon Web Services AWS project estimates?

265. Are the processes for status updates and maintenance defined?

266. What is the estimated time to complete the Amazon Web Services AWS project if status quo is maintained?

267. Has the IMS been resource-loaded and are assigned resources reasonable and available?

268. Is there a formal set of procedures supporting Issues Management?

269. Were Amazon Web Services AWS project team members involved in detailed estimating and scheduling?

270. Are any non-compliance issues that exist due to the organizations practices communicated to the organization?

271. Are metrics used to evaluate and manage Vendors?

272. Are the primary and secondary schedule tools defined?

273. Was your organizations estimating methodology being used and followed?

274. Are changes in scope (deliverable commitments) agreed to by all affected groups & individuals?

275. Why Time Management?

2.11 Activity List: Amazon Web Services AWS

276. When will the work be performed?

277. For other activities, how much delay can be tolerated?

278. What is the LF and LS for each activity?

279. How will it be performed?

280. How can the Amazon Web Services AWS project be displayed graphically to better visualize the activities?

281. Is there anything planned that doesn t need to be here?

282. What is the least expensive way to complete the Amazon Web Services AWS project within 40 weeks?

283. What is the total time required to complete the Amazon Web Services AWS project if no delays occur?

284. How much slack is available in the Amazon Web Services AWS project?

285. What did not go as well?

286. What went well?

287. How difficult will it be to do specific activities on

this Amazon Web Services AWS project?

288. How do you determine the late start (LS) for each activity?

289. How detailed should a Amazon Web Services AWS project get?

290. Where will it be performed?

291. What will be performed?

292. When do the individual activities need to start and finish?

293. Are the required resources available or need to be acquired?

2.12 Activity Attributes: Amazon Web Services AWS

294. Does the organization of the data change its meaning?

295. How difficult will it be to do specific activities on this Amazon Web Services AWS project?

296. Activity: Fair or Not Fair?

297. Would you consider either of these activities an outlier?

298. What is the organization s history in doing similar activities?

299. Were there other ways you could have organized the data to achieve similar results?

300. Have you identified the Activity Leveling Priority code value on each activity?

301. Resources to accomplish the work?

302. How many resources do you need to complete the work scope within a limit of X number of days?

303. Whats Missing?

304. How else could the items be grouped?

305. Can you re-assign any activities to another

resource to resolve an over-allocation?

306. How difficult will it be to complete specific activities on this Amazon Web Services AWS project?

307. Have constraints been applied to the start and finish milestones for the phases?

308. Activity: Whats In the Bag?

309. Whats the general pattern here?

2.13 Milestone List: Amazon Web Services AWS

310. Political effects?

311. Describe the industry you are in and the market growth opportunities. What is the market for your technology, product or service?

312. Own known vulnerabilities?

313. Timescales, deadlines and pressures?

314. How soon can the activity finish?

315. What would happen if a delivery of material was one week late?

316. Gaps in capabilities?

317. How late can each activity be finished and started?

318. Competitive advantages?

319. What is the market for your technology, product or service?

320. Sustainable financial backing?

321. Information and research?

322. Who will manage the Amazon Web Services AWS

project on a day-to-day basis?

323. What has been done so far?

324. Level of the Innovation?

325. Environmental effects?

326. Milestone pages should display the UserID of the person who added the milestone. Does a report or query exist that provides this audit information?

2.14 Network Diagram: Amazon Web Services AWS

327. What can be done concurrently?

328. Will crashing x weeks return more in benefits than it costs?

329. What to do and When?

330. Are you on time?

331. What are the Major Administrative Issues?

332. Are the required resources available?

333. What controls the start and finish of a job?

334. What is the probability of completing the Amazon Web Services AWS project in less that xx days?

335. What job or jobs could run concurrently?

336. What job or jobs precede it?

337. What are the tools?

338. Can you calculate the confidence level?

339. What is the lowest cost to complete this Amazon Web Services AWS project in xx weeks?

340. What activity must be completed immediately before this activity can start?

341. What is the completion time?

342. What must be completed before an activity can be started?

343. If a current contract exists, can you provide the vendor name, contract start, and contract expiration date?

344. Planning: who, how long, what to do?

345. If X is long, what would be the completion time if you break X into two parallel parts of y weeks and z weeks?

346. Where do you schedule uncertainty time?

2.15 Activity Resource Requirements: Amazon Web Services AWS

347. How do you handle petty cash?

348. When does Monitoring Begin?

349. Are there unresolved issues that need to be addressed?

350. Organizational Applicability?

351. Which logical relationship does the PDM use most often?

352. How many signatures do you require on a check and does this match what is in your policy and procedures?

353. What is the Work Plan Standard?

354. Why do you do that?

355. Time for overtime?

356. What are constraints that you might find during the Human Resource Planning process?

357. Other support in specific areas?

358. Do you use tools like decomposition and rolling-wave planning to produce the activity list and other outputs?

359. Anything else?

2.16 Resource Breakdown Structure: Amazon Web Services AWS

360. Any Changes from Stakeholders?

361. Which resources should be in the resource pool?

362. Who delivers the information?

363. Who will use the system?

364. What can you do to improve productivity?

365. Is Predictive Resource Analysis being done?

366. Goals for the Amazon Web Services AWS project. What is each stakeholders desired outcome for the Amazon Web Services AWS project?

367. Who will be used as a Amazon Web Services AWS project team member?

368. What is each stakeholders desired outcome for the Amazon Web Services AWS project?

369. Who needs what information?

370. What are the requirements for resource data?

371. What is the organizations history in doing similar activities?

372. What Defines a Successful Amazon Web Services

AWS project?

373. How difficult will it be to do specific activities on this Amazon Web Services AWS project?

374. Why Do you Do It?

2.17 Activity Duration Estimates: Amazon Web Services AWS

375. Describe Amazon Web Services AWS project integration management in your own words. How does Amazon Web Services AWS project integration management relate to the Amazon Web Services AWS project life cycle, stakeholders, and the other Amazon Web Services AWS project management knowledge areas?

376. Do you think many other organizations could apply this methodology, or does each organization need to create its own methodology?

377. Are resource rates available to calculate Amazon Web Services AWS project costs?

378. Are updates on work results collected and used as inputs to the performance reporting process?

379. What are the main types of goods and services being outsourced?

380. Discuss the history of modern quality management. How have experts such as Deming, Juran, Crosby, and Taguchi affected the quality movement and todays use of Six Sigma?

381. Are contractor costs, schedule and technical performance monitored throughout the Amazon Web Services AWS project?

382. If Amazon Web Services AWS project time and cost are not as important as the number of resources used each month, which is the BEST thing to do?

383. Are training needs identified when resources do not have the required skills to complete Amazon Web Services AWS project activities?

384. Are Amazon Web Services AWS project records organized, maintained, and assessable by Amazon Web Services AWS project team members?

385. How does Amazon Web Services AWS project management relate to other disciplines?

386. What is the shortest possible time it will take to complete this Amazon Web Services AWS project?

387. Is action taken to increase the effectiveness and efficiency of Amazon Web Services AWS projects?

388. Does a procedure exist to ensure the Amazon Web Services AWS project work is completed in the appropriate sequence and on time?

389. Which type of mathematical analysis is being used?

390. Which is the BEST thing to do to try to complete a Amazon Web Services AWS project two days earlier?

391. Are Amazon Web Services AWS project management tools and techniques consistently applied throughout all Amazon Web Services AWS projects?

392. What is the BEST thing to do?

393. How does poking fun at technical professionals communications skills impact the industry and educational programs?

2.18 Duration Estimating Worksheet: Amazon Web Services AWS

394. Value Pocket Identification & Quantification What Are Value Pockets?

395. Why Estimate Costs?

396. What s Next?

397. What is the probability the Amazon Web Services AWS project can be completed in 47 weeks?

398. How should ongoing costs be monitored to try to keep the Amazon Web Services AWS project within budget?

399. Is the Amazon Web Services AWS project responsive to community need?

400. Done before proceeding with this activity or what can be done concurrently?

401. How can the Amazon Web Services AWS project be displayed graphically to better visualize the activities?

402. Define the work as completely as possible. What work will be included in the Amazon Web Services AWS project?

403. When does the organization expect to be able to complete it?

404. Do any colleagues have experience with the company and/or RFPs?

405. What utility impacts are there?

406. What is Cost and Amazon Web Services AWS project Cost Management?

407. What is the least expensive way to complete the Amazon Web Services AWS project within 40 weeks?

408. Science = Process: Remember the Scientific Method?

409. What s an Average Amazon Web Services AWS project?

410. Small or Large Amazon Web Services AWS project?

2.19 Project Schedule: Amazon Web Services AWS

411. How can slack be negative?

412. Why Do you Need Schedules?

413. What documents, if any, will the subcontractor provide (eg Amazon Web Services AWS project schedule, quality plan etc)?

414. Your best shot for providing estimations how complex/how much work does the activity require?

415. How does a Amazon Web Services AWS project get to be a year late ?

416. What does that mean?

417. How effectively were issues able to be resolved without impacting the Amazon Web Services AWS project Schedule or Budget?

418. Verify that the update is accurate. Are all remaining durations correct?

419. If there are any qualifying green components to this Amazon Web Services AWS project, what portion of the total Amazon Web Services AWS project cost is green?

420. It allows the Amazon Web Services AWS project to be delivered on schedule. How Do you Use

Schedules?

421. Did the final product meet or exceed user expectations?

422. Why is software Amazon Web Services AWS project disaster so common?

423. What is Amazon Web Services AWS project Management?

424. How closely did the initial Amazon Web Services AWS project Schedule compare with the actual schedule?

425. Are procedures defined by which the Amazon Web Services AWS project schedule may be changed?

426. Did the Amazon Web Services AWS project come in under budget?

427. Understand the constraints used in preparing the schedule. Are activities connected because logic dictates the order in which others occur?

428. The WBS is developed as part of a Joint Planning session. But how do you know that youve done this right?

429. How Do you Use Schedules?

2.20 Cost Management Plan: Amazon Web Services AWS

430. Pareto diagrams, statistical sampling, flow charting or trend analysis used quality monitoring?

431. Forecasts – How will the time and resources needed to complete the Amazon Web Services AWS project be forecast?

432. Is the structure for tracking the Amazon Web Services AWS project schedule well defined and assigned to a specific individual?

433. Are the quality tools and methods identified in the Quality Plan appropriate to the Amazon Web Services AWS project?

434. Vac -variance at completion, how much over/under budget do you expect to be?

435. Is PERT / Critical Path or equivalent methodology being used?

436. Have key stakeholders been identified?

437. Are corrective actions and variances reported?

438. Have all team members been part of identifying risks?

439. Amazon Web Services AWS project Objectives?

440. What Is Amazon Web Services AWS project Management?

441. Are key risk mitigation strategies added to the Amazon Web Services AWS project schedule?

442. Is It a Amazon Web Services AWS project?

443. Are trade-offs between accepting the risk and mitigating the risk identified?

444. Is Amazon Web Services AWS project status reviewed with the steering and executive teams at appropriate intervals?

445. Have process improvement efforts been completed before requirements efforts begin?

446. Are Amazon Web Services AWS project contact logs kept up to date?

447. Milestones – What are the key dates in executing the contract plan?

448. Have Amazon Web Services AWS project management standards and procedures been identified / established and documented?

2.21 Activity Cost Estimates: Amazon Web Services AWS

449. What cost data should be used to estimate costs during the 2-year follow-up period?

450. What happens if you cannot produce the documentation for the single audit?

451. When do you enter into PPM?

452. What procedures are put in place regarding bidding and cost comparisons, if any?

453. Were sponsors and decision makers available when needed outside regularly scheduled meetings?

454. Were the tasks or work products prepared by the consultant useful?

455. Were you satisfied with the work?

456. Does the activity use a common approach or business function to deliver its results?

457. Review – what are some common errors in activities to avoid?

458. What were things that you did well, but could improve, and how?

459. How Do you Manage Cost?

460. What is Amazon Web Services AWS project Cost Management?

461. What is a Amazon Web Services AWS project Management Plan?

462. What is the activity inventory?

463. Does the activity serve a common type of customer?

464. Measurable - Are the targets measurable?

465. Maintenance Reserve?

466. Specific - Is the objective clear in terms of what, how, when, and where the situation will be changed?

467. What makes a good activity description?

2.22 Cost Estimating Worksheet: Amazon Web Services AWS

468. Is the Amazon Web Services AWS project responsive to community need?

469. What is the estimated labor cost today based upon this information?

470. What is the purpose of estimating?

471. Will the Amazon Web Services AWS project collaborate with the local community and leverage resources?

472. What happens to any remaining funds not used?

473. Is it feasible to establish a control group arrangement?

474. Identify the timeframe necessary to monitor progress and collect data to determine how the selected measure has changed?

475. What Can Be Included?

476. Ask: are others positioned to know, are others credible, and will others cooperate?

477. Who is best positioned to know and assist in identifying such factors?

478. What costs are to be estimated?

479. What will others want?

480. Does the Amazon Web Services AWS project provide innovative ways for stakeholders to overcome obstacles or deliver better outcomes?

481. What additional Amazon Web Services AWS project(s) could be initiated as a result of this Amazon Web Services AWS project?

482. How will the results be shared and to whom?

483. Can a trend be established from historical performance data on the selected measure and are the criteria for using trend analysis or forecasting methods met?

484. What info is needed?

2.23 Cost Baseline: Amazon Web Services AWS

485. Will the Amazon Web Services AWS project fail if the change request is not executed?

486. On budget?

487. Are there contingencies or conditions related to the acceptance?

488. Have the actual milestone completion dates been compared to the approved schedule?

489. If you sold 11 widgets on day, what would the affect on profits be?

490. Are you asking management for something as a result of this update?

491. What does it mean to say a task is 75% complete after 3 months?

492. Has the Amazon Web Services AWS project documentation been archived or otherwise disposed as described in the Amazon Web Services AWS project communication plan?

493. Is request in line with priorities?

494. What would some of the life cycle costs be?

495. Verify business objectives. Are others

appropriate, and well-articulated?

496. What deliverables come first?

497. Does the suggested change request represent a desired enhancement to the products functionality?

498. Is there anything you need from upper management in order to be successful?

499. How likely is it to go wrong?

500. What s the reality?

501. How will cost estimates be used?

502. Has the Amazon Web Services AWS project (or Amazon Web Services AWS project phase) been evaluated against each objective established in the product description and Integrated Amazon Web Services AWS project Plan?

503. Does the suggested change request seem to represent a necessary enhancement to the product?

504. Definition of done can be traced back to the definitions of what are you providing to the customer in terms of deliverables?

2.24 Quality Management Plan: Amazon Web Services AWS

505. Meet how often?

506. What are your results for key measures/indicators of accomplishment of organizational strategy?

507. How do you decide what information needs to be recorded?

508. What are the established criteria that sampling / testing data are compared against?

509. What is quality and how will you ensure it?

510. Is the amount of effort justified by the anticipated value of forming a new process?

511. How do you decide who is responsible for signing the data reports?

512. How do you ensure that your sampling methods and procedures meet your data quality objectives?

513. Are you meeting our customers expectations consistently?

514. Have all stakeholders been identified?

515. How does your organization decide what to measure?

516. Have you eliminated all duplicative tasks or manual efforts, where appropriate?

517. What key performance indicators does your organization use to measure, manage, and improve key processes?

518. Who is responsible?

519. How many Amazon Web Services AWS project staff does this specific process affect?

520. How do you ensure that protocols are up to date?

521. What procedures are used to determine if you use, and the number of split, replicate or duplicate samples taken at a site?

522. Explain the procedures used to verify the data quality of the data being reviewed?

523. Have Amazon Web Services AWS project management standards and procedures been established and documented?

524. How long do you retain data?

2.25 Quality Metrics: Amazon Web Services AWS

525. Is material complete (and does it meet the standards)?

526. Is there a set of procedures to capture, analyze and act on quality metrics?

527. What is the timeline to meet our goal?

528. How should customers provide input?

529. Which are the right metrics to use?

530. Product Availability ?

531. Are quality metrics defined?

532. How do you calculate such metrics?

533. What metrics are important and most beneficial to measure?

534. Is the reporting frequency appropriate?

535. Who is willing to lead?

536. What forces exist that would cause them to change?

537. Has trace of defects been initiated?

538. Which report did you use to create the data you are submitting?

539. What does this tell us?

540. Filter Visualizations of Interest?

541. Is there alignment within your company on definitions?

542. What level of statistical confidence do you use?

543. Which data do others need in one place to target areas of improvement?

544. How do you measure?

2.26 Process Improvement Plan: Amazon Web Services AWS

545. What is the return on investment?

546. To elicit goal statements, do you ask a question such as, What do you want to achieve?

547. Have the supporting tools been developed or acquired?

548. Management commitment at all levels?

549. Have storage and access mechanisms and procedures been determined?

550. If a Process Improvement Framework Is Being Used, Which Elements Will Help the Problems and Goals Listed?

551. Are there forms and procedures to collect and record the data?

552. Has a process guide to collect the data been developed?

553. Has the time line required to move measurement results from the points of collection to databases or users been established?

554. Does our process ensure quality?

555. Are you meeting the quality standards?

556. Are you following the quality standards?

557. Everyone agrees on what process improvement is, right?

558. Are you Making Progress on the Goals?

559. Who should prepare the process improvement action plan?

560. Have the frequency of collection and the points in the process where measurements will be made been determined?

561. What Is the Test-Cycle Concept?

562. The motive is determined by asking, Why do I want to achieve this goal?

563. Where do you focus?

564. What personnel are the change agents for your initiative?

2.27 Responsibility Assignment Matrix: Amazon Web Services AWS

565. Those responsible for the establishment of budgets and assignment of resources for overhead performance?

566. How do you manage remotely to staff in other Divisions?

567. What is the purpose of assigning and documenting responsibility?

568. Are too many reports done in writing instead of verbally?

569. Are people encouraged to bring up issues?

570. What expertise is not available in your department?

571. Performance to date and material commitment?

572. Do work packages consist of discrete tasks which are adequately described?

573. How many hours by each staff member/rate?

574. Do You Know How Your People are Allocated?

575. Is all contract work included in the CWBS?

576. Identify potential or actual budget-based and

time-based schedule variances?

577. Contract line items and end items?

578. Authorization to proceed with all authorized work?

579. Which resource planning tool provides information on resource responsibility and accountability?

580. Are the bases and rates for allocating costs from each indirect pool consistently applied?

581. The staff interests – is the group or the person interested in working for this Amazon Web Services AWS project?

582. Is work properly classified as measured effort, LOE, or apportioned effort and appropriately separated?

2.28 Roles and Responsibilities: Amazon Web Services AWS

583. Implementation of actions: Who are the responsible units?

584. What are my major roles and responsibilities in the area of performance measurement and assessment?

585. Are the quality assurance functions and related roles and responsibilities clearly defined?

586. What areas of supervision are challenging for you?

587. Are our policies supportive of a culture of quality data?

588. Are Amazon Web Services AWS project team roles and responsibilities identified and documented?

589. What expectations were NOT met?

590. Where are you most strong as a supervisor?

591. Does the team have access to and ability to use data analysis tools?

592. Who is involved?

593. Who is responsible for each task?

594. Concern: where are you limited or have no authority, where you cant influence?

595. Are governance roles and responsibilities documented?

596. What should you do now to prepare for your career 5+ years from now?

597. Are Amazon Web Services AWS project team roles and responsibilities identified and documented?

598. Is there a training program in place for stakeholders covering expectations, roles and responsibilities and any addition knowledge others need to be good stakeholders?

599. Does our vision/mission support a culture of quality data?

600. Are our budgets supportive of a culture of quality data?

601. What is working well within your organizations performance management system?

2.29 Human Resource Management Plan: Amazon Web Services AWS

602. Is an industry recognized support tool(s) being used for Amazon Web Services AWS project scheduling & tracking?

603. Has the business need been clearly defined?

604. Were the budget estimates reasonable?

605. Are changes in deliverable commitments agreed to by all affected groups & individuals?

606. Are Vendor invoices audited for accuracy before payment?

607. Has a capability assessment been conducted?

608. Is stakeholder involvement adequate?

609. Are staff skills known and available for each task?

610. Are the schedule estimates reasonable given the Amazon Web Services AWS project?

611. Were decisions made in a timely manner?

612. Were escalated issues resolved promptly?

613. Has the Amazon Web Services AWS project scope been baselined?

614. Are Amazon Web Services AWS project team members committed fulltime?

615. Were Amazon Web Services AWS project team members involved in detailed estimating and scheduling?

616. Are meeting objectives identified for each meeting?

617. Are schedule deliverables actually delivered?

2.30 Communications Management Plan: Amazon Web Services AWS

618. Are there common objectives between the team and the stakeholder?

619. Is there an important stakeholder who is actively opposed and will not receive messages?

620. Conflict Resolution -which method when?

621. Are there too many who have an interest in some aspect of your work?

622. Which team member will work with each stakeholder?

623. Do you feel a register helps?

624. Do you have members of your team responsible for certain stakeholders?

625. Are the stakeholders getting the information others need, are others consulted, are concerns addressed?

626. Is the stakeholder role recognized by the organization?

627. Who needs to know and how much?

628. What approaches do you use?

629. What to learn?

630. Who will use or be affected by the result of a Amazon Web Services AWS project?

631. Do you prepare stakeholder engagement plans?

632. Are you constantly rushing from meeting to meeting?

633. What communications method?

634. What does the stakeholder need from the team?

635. What help do you and your team need from the stakeholder?

636. How is this initiative related to other portfolios, programs, or Amazon Web Services AWS projects?

637. Why Do you Manage Communications?

2.31 Risk Management Plan: Amazon Web Services AWS

638. Risks should be identified during which phase of Amazon Web Services AWS project management life cycle?

639. Premium on reliability of product?

640. What risks are necessary to achieve success?

641. What are IT-specific requirements?

642. Is a software Amazon Web Services AWS project management tool available?

643. What is the impact to the Amazon Web Services AWS project if the item is not resolved in a timely fashion?

644. Does the Amazon Web Services AWS project team have experience with the technology to be implemented?

645. Does the Amazon Web Services AWS project have the authority and ability to avoid the risk?

646. Which is an input to the risk management process?

647. Risk Probability and Impact: How will the probabilities and impacts of risk items be assessed?

648. How much risk protection can you afford?

649. What would you do?

650. Do benefits and chances of success outweigh potential damage if success is not attained?

651. How is Implementation of Risk Actions Performed?

652. How Is The Audit Profession Changing?

653. User Involvement: Do I have the right users?

654. Are people attending meetings and doing work?

655. Could others have been better mitigated?

656. Why Is Product Liability a Serious Issue?

657. Is the customer willing to participate in reviews?

2.32 Risk Register: Amazon Web Services AWS

658. Manageability – Have mitigations to the risk been identified?

659. Are there any knock-on effects/impact on any of the other areas?

660. Assume the risk event or situation happens, what would the impact be?

661. People risk -Are people with appropriate skills available to help complete the Amazon Web Services AWS project?

662. How are Risks Graded?

663. What are the main aims, objectives of the policy, strategy, or service and the intended outcomes?

664. What further options might be available for responding to the risk?

665. Assume the event happens, what is the Most Likely impact?

666. Have other controls and solutions been implemented in other services which could be applied as an alternative to additional funding?

667. What is a Risk?

668. Budget and Schedule: What are the estimated costs and schedules for performing risk-related activities?

669. How could such Risk affect the Amazon Web Services AWS project in terms of cost and schedule?

670. Why would you develop a risk register?

671. What action, if any, has been taken to respond to the risk?

672. What are you going to do to limit the Amazon Web Services AWS projects risk exposure due to the identified risks?

673. Are our objectives at risk?

674. What has changed since the last period?

675. Preventative actions - planned actions to reduce the likelihood a risk will occur and/or reduce the seriousness should it occur. What should you do now?

676. Who needs to know about this?

677. What will be done?

2.33 Probability and Impact Assessment: Amazon Web Services AWS

678. What significant shift will occur in governmental policies, laws, and regulations pertaining to specific industries?

679. What is the impact if the risk does occur?

680. Do requirements demand the use of new analysis, design, or testing methods?

681. Are the best people available?

682. Are some people working on multiple Amazon Web Services AWS projects?

683. Are team members trained in the use of the tools?

684. What is the experience (performance, attitude, business ethics, etc.) in the past with contractors?

685. Prioritized components/features?

686. Do you manage the process through use of metrics?

687. Anticipated volatility of the requirements?

688. Which of your Amazon Web Services AWS projects should be selected when compared with

other Amazon Web Services AWS projects?

689. Is there additional information that would make you more confident about your analysis?

690. Is the customer technically sophisticated in the product area?

691. Is the customer willing to establish rapid communication links with the developer?

692. Do you use diagramming techniques to show cause and effect?

693. Do you use any methods to analyze risks?

694. Can you avoid altogether some things that might go wrong?

695. Are there new risks that mitigation strategies might introduce?

2.34 Probability and Impact Matrix: Amazon Web Services AWS

696. Is the process supported by tools?

697. Economic to take on the Amazon Web Services AWS project?

698. How would you assess the risk management process in the Amazon Web Services AWS project?

699. Can it be enlarged by drawing people from other areas of the organization?

700. What will the damage be?

701. Workarounds are determined during which step of risk management?

702. What are the uncertainties associated with the technology selected for the Amazon Web Services AWS project?

703. Is security a central objective?

704. Has something like this been done before?

705. Are enough people available?

706. How can you understand and diagnose risks and identify sources?

707. Do you train all developers in the process?

708. Is the present organizational structure for handling the Amazon Web Services AWS project sufficient?

709. What is the best method for analysing the risks for different types of Amazon Web Services AWS projects?

710. What things might go wrong?

711. Does the customer understand the software process?

712. Is a software Amazon Web Services AWS project management tool available?

713. What should be the level of difficulty in handling the technology?

2.35 Risk Data Sheet: Amazon Web Services AWS

714. Type of Risk Identified?

715. Is the data sufficiently specified in terms of the type of failure being analysed, and its frequency or probability?

716. What are you weak at and therefore need to do better?

717. What were the Causes that contributed?

718. Are new hazards created?

719. How reliable is the data source?

720. What is the environment within which you operate (social trends, economic, community values, broad based participation, national directions etc.)?

721. How can hazards be reduced?

722. Has a sensitivity analysis been carried out?

723. What Do you Know?

724. What is the duration of infection (the length of time the host is infected with the organizm) in a normal healthy human host?

725. What can YOU do?

726. Will revised controls lead to tolerable risk levels?

727. Who has a vested interest in how you perform as an organization (our stakeholders)?

728. What was Measured?

729. What is the chance that it will happen?

730. Potential for Recurrence?

731. What are the main threats to our existence?

732. During work activities could hazards exist?

733. What can happen?

2.36 Procurement Management Plan: Amazon Web Services AWS

734. Public engagement – Did you get it right?

735. Has a Quality Assurance Plan been developed for the Amazon Web Services AWS project?

736. Are any non-compliance issues that exist communicated to the organization?

737. Have the procedures for identifying budget variances been followed?

738. Are status reports received per the Amazon Web Services AWS project Plan?

739. Is the communication plan being followed?

740. Are milestone deliverables effectively tracked and compared to Amazon Web Services AWS project plan?

741. If standardized procurement documents are needed, where can others be found?

742. Does the detailed work plan match the complexity of tasks with the capabilities of personnel?

743. Is the assigned Amazon Web Services AWS project manager a PMP (Certified Amazon Web Services AWS project manager) and experienced?

744. What areas does the group agree are the biggest success on the Amazon Web Services AWS project?

745. Based on your Amazon Web Services AWS project communication management plan, what worked well?

746. Are the people assigned to the Amazon Web Services AWS project sufficiently qualified?

747. Is the schedule updated on a periodic basis?

748. Are decisions made in a timely manner?

749. Are parking lot items captured?

750. Were Amazon Web Services AWS project team members involved in detailed estimating and scheduling?

2.37 Source Selection Criteria: Amazon Web Services AWS

751. How can solicitation Schedules be improved to yield more effective price competition?

752. When should debriefings be held and how should they be scheduled?

753. Is a cost realism analysis used?

754. Do you prepare an independent cost estimate?

755. What are the requirements for publicizing a RFP?

756. Do you discuss all weaknesses, significant weaknesses, and deficiencies?

757. What evidence should be provided regarding proposal evaluations?

758. What is the role of counsel in the procurement process?

759. What Should Be Discussed?

760. How should oral presentations be evaluated?

761. In order of importance, which evaluation criteria are the most critical to the determination of your overall rating?

762. What are the steps in performing a cost/tech

tradeoff?

763. How firm are proposed quotes/prices?

764. How do you encourage efficiency and consistency?

765. What documentation is necessary regarding electronic communications?

766. Have team members been adequately trained?

767. When is it appropriate to issue a DRFP?

768. What management structure does the organization consider as optimal for performing the contract?

769. How long will it take for the purchase cost to be the same as the lease cost?

770. What are the special considerations for preaward debriefings?

2.38 Stakeholder Management Plan: Amazon Web Services AWS

771. If a problem has been detected, what tools can be used to determine a root cause?

772. How will you engage this stakeholder and gain their commitment?

773. Has the budget been baselined?

774. Do you know what your customers expectations are regarding this process?

775. Is there general agreement & acceptance of the current status and progress of the Amazon Web Services AWS project?

776. What are the criteria for selecting suppliers of off the shelf products?

777. Is Amazon Web Services AWS project status reviewed with the steering and executive teams at appropriate intervals?

778. Are there procedures in place to effectively manage interdependencies with other Amazon Web Services AWS projects / systems?

779. Is it possible to track all classes of Amazon Web Services AWS project work (e.g. scheduled, un-scheduled, defect repair, etc.)?

780. Are risk triggers captured?

781. At what point will the Amazon Web Services AWS project be closed and what will be done to formally close the Amazon Web Services AWS project?

782. Has an organization readiness assessment been conducted?

783. Has a Resource Management Plan been created?

784. Are adequate resources provided for the quality assurance function?

785. Are procurement deliverables arriving on time and to specification?

786. What is the general purpose in defining responsibilities of those affiliated with the Amazon Web Services AWS project?

787. Where to Get Additional Help?

2.39 Change Management Plan: Amazon Web Services AWS

788. What does a resilient organization look like?

789. When does it make sense to customize?

790. What are the specific target groups / audience that will be impacted by this change?

791. Would you need to tailor a special message for each segment of the audience?

792. Is there a support model for this application and are the details available for distribution?

793. Has the relevant business unit been notified of installation and support requirements?

794. Is there a software application relevant to this deliverable?

795. Who should be involved in developing a change management strategy?

796. Do you need new systems?

797. Who in the business it includes?

798. What are the training strategies?

799. Has the target training audience been identified and nominated?

800. What is the most positive interpretation it can receive?

801. Identify the current level of skills and knowledge and behaviours of the group that will be impacted on. What prerequisite knowledge do these groups need?

802. What new behaviours are required?

803. Has an Information & communications plan been developed?

804. How will you deal with anger about the restricting of communications due to confidentiality considerations?

805. Who is the audience for change management activities?

806. What are the key change management success metrics?

807. What are you trying to achieve as a result of communication?

3.0 Executing Process Group: Amazon Web Services AWS

808. When will the Amazon Web Services AWS project be done?

809. How well did the chosen processes fit the needs of the Amazon Web Services AWS project?

810. What Amazon Web Services AWS projects and services are in the portfolio of your organization?

811. How many different communication channels does the Amazon Web Services AWS project team have?

812. How well defined and documented were the Amazon Web Services AWS project management processes you chose to use?

813. Does software appear easy to learn?

814. What communication items need improvement?

815. How well did the chosen processes produce the expected results?

816. What type of people would you want on your team?

817. Is activity definition the first process involved in Amazon Web Services AWS project time management?

818. If a risk event occurs, what will you do?

819. How well did the team follow the chosen processes?

820. What is the difference between using brainstorming and the Delphi technique for risk identification?

821. It under budget or over budget?

822. In what way has the programme come up with innovative measures for problem-solving?

823. How will you avoid scope creep?

824. How does a Amazon Web Services AWS project life cycle differ from a product life cycle?

825. When is the appropriate time to bring the scorecard to Board meetings?

826. What are the main types of contracts if you do decide to outsource?

3.1 Team Member Status Report: Amazon Web Services AWS

827. Does the organization have the means (staff, money, contract, etc.) to produce or to acquire the product, good, or service?

828. Why is it to be done?

829. Do you have an Enterprise Amazon Web Services AWS project Management Office (EPMO)?

830. Is there evidence that staff is taking a more professional approach toward management of the organizations Amazon Web Services AWS projects?

831. The problem with Reward & Recognition Programs is that the truly deserving people all too often get left out. How can you make it practical?

832. How it is to be done?

833. Will the staff do training or is that done by a third party?

834. When a teams productivity and success depend on collaboration and the efficient flow of information, what generally fails them?

835. Are the organization's Amazon Web Services AWS projects more successful over time?

836. How does this product, good, or service meet the

needs of the Amazon Web Services AWS project and the organization as a whole?

837. Does the product, good, or service already exist within the organization?

838. How will Resource Planning be done?

839. How much risk is involved?

840. Are the products of the organization's Amazon Web Services AWS projects meeting their customer's objectives?

841. Does every department have to have a Amazon Web Services AWS project Manager on staff?

842. How can you make it practical?

843. What specific interest groups do you have in place?

844. What is to be done?

845. Are the attitudes of staff regarding Amazon Web Services AWS project work improving?

3.2 Change Request: Amazon Web Services AWS

846. What are the basic mechanics of the Change Advisory Board (CAB)?

847. Which requirements attributes affect the risk to reliability the most?

848. Who Will Perform the Change?

849. What mechanism is used to appraise others of changes that are made?

850. How Fast Will Change Requests be Approved?

851. Will all change requests be unconditionally tracked through this process?

852. What is the relationship between requirements attributes and attributes like complexity and size?

853. Will new change requests be acknowledged in a timely manner?

854. Screen shots or attachments included in a Change Request?

855. What are the duties of the change control team?

856. Are there requirements attributes that are strongly related to the complexity and size?

857. Why control change across the life cycle?

858. Describe how modifications, enhancements, defects and/or deficiencies shall be notified (e.g. Problem Reports, Change Requests etc) and managed. Detail warranty and/or maintenance periods?

859. Can static requirements change attributes like the size of the change be used to predict reliability in execution?

860. Are there requirements attributes that are strongly related to the occurrence of defects and failures?

861. Will this change conflict with other requirements changes (e.g., lead to conflicting operational scenarios)?

862. Who has responsibility for approving and ranking changes?

863. Change Request Coordination ?

864. Has a formal technical review been conducted to assess technical correctness?

865. Where Do Changes Come From?

3.3 Change Log: Amazon Web Services AWS

866. When was the request approved?

867. How does this change affect scope?

868. Is the change backward compatible without limitations?

869. How does this relate to the standards developed for specific business processes?

870. When was the request submitted?

871. Is the change request within Amazon Web Services AWS project scope?

872. Is the submitted change a new change or a modification of a previously approved change?

873. Should a more thorough impact analysis be conducted?

874. Is this a mandatory replacement?

875. How does this change affect the timeline of the schedule?

876. Is the requested change request a result of changes in other Amazon Web Services AWS project(s)?

877. Who initiated the change request?

878. Do the described changes impact on the integrity or security of the system?

879. Is the change request open, closed or pending?

880. Will the Amazon Web Services AWS project fail if the change request is not executed?

3.4 Decision Log: Amazon Web Services AWS

881. What alternatives/risks were considered?

882. Do strategies and tactics aimed at less than full control reduce the costs of management or simply shift the cost burden?

883. Is everything working as expected?

884. What makes you different or better than others companies selling the same thing?

885. At what point in time does loss become unacceptable?

886. Who will be given a copy of this document and where will it be kept?

887. Decision-making process; how will the team make decisions?

888. How does provision of information, both in terms of content and presentation, influence acceptance of alternative strategies?

889. What was the rationale for the decision?

890. So, what is the line where eDiscovery ends and document review begins?

891. How effective is maintaining the log at

facilitating organizational learning?

892. What is your overall strategy for quality control / quality assurance procedures?

893. Is your opponent open to a non-traditional workflow, or will it likely challenge anything you do?

894. How do you define success?

895. With whom was the decision shared or discussed?

896. Linked to original objective?

897. Adversarial Environment. Is your opponent open to a non-traditional workflow, or will it likely challenge anything you do?

898. How does the use a Decision Support System influence the strategies/tactics or costs?

899. What is the average size of your matters in an applicable measurement?

900. Behaviors; what are guidelines that the team has identified that will assist them with getting the most out of their team meetings?

3.5 Quality Audit: Amazon Web Services AWS

901. How does the organization know that its teaching activities (and staff learning) are effectively and constructively enhanced by its activities?

902. How does the organization know that its staff embody the core knowledge, skills and characteristics for which it wishes to be recognized?

903. Is Quality Audit a prerequisite for Program Accreditation or Program Recognition?

904. How does the organization know that its support services planning and management systems are appropriately effective and constructive?

905. How does the organization know that its systems for meeting staff extracurricular learning support requirements are appropriately effective and constructive?

906. Is progress against the intentions measurable?

907. A judgment has to be made as to whether a particular practice is good or poor or otherwise. How does one decide on a practice?

908. How does the organization know that its management system is appropriately effective and constructive?

909. What is the collective experience of the team to be assigned to an audit?

910. How does the organization know that its system for managing intellectual property issues is appropriately effective, constructive and fair?

911. Is there a written procedure for receiving materials?

912. Does everyone know what they are supposed to be doing, how and why?

913. What does an analysis of the organizations staff profile suggest in terms of its planning, and how is this being addressed?

914. Have the risks associated with the intentions been identified, analysed and appropriate responses developed?

915. What does an analysis of an organizations staff profile suggest in terms of its planning, and how is this being addressed?

916. How do you indicate the extent to which your personnel would be expected to contribute to the work effort?

917. Does the organization have set of goals, objectives, strategies and targets that are clearly understood by the Board and staff?

918. How does the organization know that its system for ensuring that its training activities are appropriately resourced and support is appropriately

effective and constructive?

919. It is inappropriate to seek information about the Audit Panels preliminary views including questions like why do you ask that?

920. How does the organization know that its system for commercializing research outputs is appropriately effective and constructive?

3.6 Team Directory: Amazon Web Services AWS

921. Who will report Amazon Web Services AWS project status to all stakeholders?

922. Process Decisions: Do job conditions warrant additional actions to collect job information and document on-site activity?

923. Process Decisions: Which organizational elements and which individuals will be assigned management functions?

924. How and in what format should information be presented?

925. Why is the work necessary?

926. How does the team resolve conflicts and ensure tasks are completed?

927. Is construction on schedule?

928. Does a Amazon Web Services AWS project team directory list all resources assigned to the Amazon Web Services AWS project?

929. Have you decided when to celebrate the Amazon Web Services AWS projects completion date?

930. Who are the Team Members?

931. Timing: when do the effects of communication take place?

932. How will you accomplish and manage the objectives?

933. How do unidentified risks impact the outcome of the Amazon Web Services AWS project?

934. Who should receive information (all stakeholders)?

935. Decisions: Is the most suitable form of contract being used?

936. Where will the product be used and/or delivered or built when appropriate?

937. Who will be the stakeholders on your next Amazon Web Services AWS project?

938. Process Decisions: Are there any statutory or regulatory issues relevant to the timely execution of work?

939. When does information need to be distributed?

3.7 Team Operating Agreement: Amazon Web Services AWS

940. How will you resolve conflict efficiently and respectfully?

941. Do you record meetings for those unable to attend?

942. Why does the organization want to participate in teaming?

943. Do you begin with a question to engage everyone?

944. Did you draft the meeting agenda?

945. Do you upload presentation materials in advance and test the technology?

946. Do team members reside in more than two countries?

947. To whom do you deliver our services?

948. What resources can be provided for the team in terms of equipment, space, time for training, protected time and space for meetings, and travel allowances?

949. Are there the right people on your team?

950. Do you send out the agenda and meeting

materials in advance?

951. How will group handle unplanned absences?

952. What is the number of cases currently teamed?

953. Did you delegate tasks such as taking meeting minutes, presenting a topic and soliciting input?

954. Do team members need to frequently communicate as a full group to make timely decisions?

955. Does your team need access to all documents and information at all times?

956. What are some potential sources of conflict among team members?

957. What is Culture?

958. Do you prevent individuals from dominating the meeting?

959. Are there influences outside the team that may affect performance, and if so, have you identified and addressed them?

3.8 Team Performance Assessment: Amazon Web Services AWS

960. To what degree does the team possess adequate membership to achieve its ends?

961. To what degree are fresh input and perspectives systematically caught and added (for example, through information and analysis, new members, and senior sponsors)?

962. To what degree does the teams approach to its work allow for modification and improvement over time?

963. If you have criticized someones work for method variance in your role as reviewer, what was the circumstance?

964. What are Teams?

965. To what degree are the goals ambitious?

966. To what degree can team members meet frequently enough to accomplish the teams ends?

967. To what degree are the goals realistic?

968. To what degree are the teams goals and objectives clear, simple, and measurable?

969. To what degree is there a sense that only the team can succeed?

970. To what degree is the team cognizant of small wins to be celebrated along the way?

971. How do you encourage members to learn from each other?

972. How much interpersonal friction is there in your team?

973. Does more radicalness mean more perceived benefits?

974. To what degree does the teams purpose contain themes that are particularly meaningful and memorable?

975. To what degree are the skill areas critical to team performance present?

976. To what degree are the relative importance and priority of the goals clear to all team members?

977. To what degree do team members frequently explore the teams purpose and its implications?

978. To what degree can the team ensure that all members are individually and jointly accountable for the teams purpose, goals, approach, and work-products?

979. To what degree can all members engage in open and interactive discussions?

3.9 Team Member Performance Assessment: Amazon Web Services AWS

980. What future plans (e.g., modifications) do you have for your program?

981. How do you start collaborating?

982. Does statute or regulation require the job responsibility?

983. What happens if a team member receives a Rating of Unsatisfactory?

984. What is the Business Management Oversight Process?

985. Do the goals support the organizations goals?

986. What were the challenges that resulted for training and assessment?

987. What variables that affect team members achievement are within your control?

988. What evidence supports your decision-making?

989. How do you currently explain your results in the teams achievement?

990. Is it clear how goals will be accomplished?

991. How is the timing of assessments organized (e.g., pre/post-test, single point during training, multiple reassessment during training)?

992. How often are assessments to be conducted?

993. What are they responsible for?

994. What are the evaluation strategies (e.g., reaction, learning, behavior, results) used. What evaluation results did you have?

995. How do you implement Cost Reduction?

996. What steps have you taken to improve performance?

3.10 Issue Log: Amazon Web Services AWS

997. What approaches to you feel are the best ones to use?

998. Which stakeholders are thought leaders, influences, or early adopters?

999. What is a change?

1000. Are the Amazon Web Services AWS project Issues uniquely identified, including to which product they refer?

1001. How much time does it take to do it?

1002. How do you reply to this question; I am new here and managing this major program. How do you suggest I build my network?

1003. What is the status of the issue?

1004. Who is the issue assigned to?

1005. Are there potential barriers between the team and the stakeholder?

1006. Persistence; will users learn a work around or will they be bothered every time?

1007. Who were proponents/opponents?

1008. How often do you engage with stakeholders?

1009. Who reported the issue?

1010. Who have you worked with in past, similar initiatives?

1011. Can an impact cause deviation beyond team, stage or Amazon Web Services AWS project tolerances?

1012. Who are the members of the governing body?

1013. Why Do you Manage Human Resources?

4.0 Monitoring and Controlling Process Group: Amazon Web Services AWS

1014. Did the Amazon Web Services AWS project team have the right skills?

1015. Did you implement the program as designed?

1016. What kinds of things in particular are you looking for data on?

1017. How is Agile Amazon Web Services AWS project Management Done?

1018. What were things that you did very well and want to do the same again on the next Amazon Web Services AWS project?

1019. Feasibility: How much money, time, and effort can you put into this?

1020. Mitigate. What will you do to minimize the impact should a risk event occur?

1021. Accuracy: What design will lead to accurate information?

1022. What areas were overlooked on this Amazon Web Services AWS project?

1023. What input will you be required to provide the Amazon Web Services AWS project team?

1024. A Amazon Web Services AWS project management team of two has 8 key stakeholders to work with. How many potential communications channels exist on the Amazon Web Services AWS project?

1025. What is the expected monetary value of the Amazon Web Services AWS project?

1026. Who needs to be involved in the planning?

1027. Is the verbiage used appropriate and understandable?

1028. Propriety: Who needs to be involved in the evaluation to be ethical?

1029. How will staff learn how to use the deliverables?

1030. If no change, where should you look for problems?

1031. Contingency planning. If a risk event occurs, what will you do?

1032. Is it what was agreed upon?

4.1 Project Performance Report: Amazon Web Services AWS

1033. How can Amazon Web Services AWS project Sustainability be Maintained?

1034. To what degree does the funding match the requirement?

1035. To what degree does the informal organization make use of individual resources and meet individual needs?

1036. To what degree do team members articulate the team's work approach?

1037. To what degree do team members frequently explore the team's purpose and its implications?

1038. To what degree do the goals specify concrete team work products?

1039. To what degree does the team's approach to its work allow for modification and improvement over time?

1040. To what degree are the demands of the task compatible with and converge with the mission and functions of the formal organization?

1041. To what degree can team members meet frequently enough to accomplish the team's ends?

1042. To what degree will team members, individually and collectively, commit time to help themselves and others learn and develop skills?

1043. To what degree does the team's purpose constitute a broader, deeper aspiration than just accomplishing short-term goals?

1044. To what degree are the team's goals and objectives clear, simple, and measurable?

1045. To what degree can team members frequently and easily communicate with one another?

1046. To what degree is there centralized control of information sharing?

1047. What degree are the relative importance and priority of the goals clear to all team members?

1048. To what degree does the team's work approach provide opportunity for members to engage in open interaction?

4.2 Variance Analysis: Amazon Web Services AWS

1049. What are the direct labor dollars and/or hours?

1050. How have the setting and use of standards changed over time?

1051. Are records maintained to show how undistributed budgets are controlled?

1052. Are the overhead pools formally and adequately identified?

1053. Are there changes in the direct base to which overhead costs are allocated?

1054. Are records maintained to show how management reserves are used?

1055. Does the accounting system provide a basis for auditing records of direct costs chargeable to the contract?

1056. What is the incurrence of actual indirect costs in excess of budgets, by element of expense?

1057. How does the monthly budget compare to the actual experience?

1058. Are indirect costs charged to the appropriate indirect pools and incurring organization?

1059. Did a new competitor enter the market?

1060. Does the contractors system provide unit or lot costs when applicable?

1061. How does your company measure performance?

1062. Is the market likely to continue to grow at this rate next year?

1063. How are material, labor, and overhead variances calculated and recorded?

1064. How do you evaluate the impact of schedule changes, work around, et?

1065. How does the use of a single conversion element (rather than the traditional labor and overhead elements) affect standard costing?

1066. What is your organizations rationale for sharing expenses and services between business segments?

4.3 Earned Value Status: Amazon Web Services AWS

1067. Verification is a process of ensuring that the developed system satisfies the stakeholders agreements and specifications; Are you building the product right? What do you verify?

1068. When is it going to finish?

1069. Earned Value can be used in almost any Amazon Web Services AWS project situation and in almost any Amazon Web Services AWS project environment. It may be used on large Amazon Web Services AWS projects, medium sized Amazon Web Services AWS projects, tiny Amazon Web Services AWS projects (in cut-down form), complex and simple Amazon Web Services AWS projects and in any market sector. Some people, of course, know all about earned value, they have used it for years - but perhaps not as effectively as they could have?

1070. Are you hitting your Amazon Web Services AWS projects targets?

1071. How much is it going to cost by the finish?

1072. Where are your problem areas?

1073. Where is Evidence-based Earned Value in your organization reported?

1074. How does this compare with other Amazon Web

Services AWS projects?

1075. If earned value management (EVM) is so good in determining the true status of a Amazon Web Services AWS project and Amazon Web Services AWS project its completion, why is it that hardly any one uses it in information systems related Amazon Web Services AWS projects?

1076. Validation is a process of ensuring that the developed system will actually achieve the stakeholders desired outcomes; Are you building the right product? What do you validate?

1077. What is the unit of forecast value?

4.4 Risk Audit: Amazon Web Services AWS

1078. Does the implementation method matter?

1079. Does the adoption of a business risk audit approach change internal control documentation and testing practices?

1080. Does your organization have a process for meeting its ongoing taxation obligations?

1081. Will safety checks of personal equipment supplied by competitors be conducted?

1082. What expertise do auditors need to generate effective business-level risk assessments, and to what extent do auditors currently possess those attributes?

1083. Are end-users enthusiastically committed to the Amazon Web Services AWS project and the system/product to be built?

1084. Is all required equipment available?

1085. Are risk management strategies documented?

1086. What effect would a better risk management program have had?

1087. Which assets are important?

1088. How risk averse are you?

1089. How can the strategy fail/achieved?

1090. Do you have an understanding of insurance claims processes?

1091. Does your organization communicate regularly and effectively with its members?

1092. Do you have a clear plan for the future that describes what you want to do and how you are going to do it?

1093. How effective are your risk controls?

1094. Do you meet the legislative requirements (for example PAYG, super contributions) for paid employees?

1095. Is there a screening process that will ensure all participants have the fitness and skills required to safely participate?

4.5 Contractor Status Report: Amazon Web Services AWS

1096. Describe how often regular updates are made to the proposed solution. Are these regular updates included in the standard maintenance plan?

1097. How is Risk Transferred?

1098. What was the budget or estimated cost for your companys services?

1099. How long have you been using the services?

1100. What are the minimum and optimal bandwidth requirements for the proposed soluiton?

1101. Are there contractual transfer concerns?

1102. What was the final actual cost?

1103. What was the overall budget or estimated cost?

1104. Who can list a Amazon Web Services AWS project as company experience, the company or a previous employee of the company?

1105. If applicable; describe your standard schedule for new software version releases. Are new software version releases included in the standard maintenance plan?

1106. What process manages the contracts?

1107. How does the proposed individual meet each requirement?

1108. What is the average response time for answering a support call?

1109. What was the actual budget or estimated cost for your companys services?

4.6 Formal Acceptance: Amazon Web Services AWS

1110. How does your team plan to obtain formal acceptance on your Amazon Web Services AWS project?

1111. Who supplies data?

1112. Does it do what Amazon Web Services AWS project team said it would?

1113. Do you perform formal acceptance or burn-in tests?

1114. Was the sponsor/customer satisfied?

1115. Was business value realized?

1116. Did the Amazon Web Services AWS project manager and team act in a professional and ethical manner?

1117. What function(s) does it fill or meet?

1118. Was the Amazon Web Services AWS project goal achieved?

1119. How well did the team follow the methodology?

1120. Does it do what client said it would?

1121. Who would use it?

1122. Do you buy pre-configured systems or build your own configuration?

1123. Is formal acceptance of the Amazon Web Services AWS project product documented and distributed?

1124. What was done right?

1125. What features, practices, and processes proved to be strengths or weaknesses?

1126. What is the Acceptance Management Process?

1127. What are the requirements against which to test, Who will execute?

1128. Do you buy-in installation services?

1129. What can you do better next time?

5.0 Closing Process Group: Amazon Web Services AWS

1130. Who are the Amazon Web Services AWS project stakeholders?

1131. Did you do what you said you were going to do?

1132. Was the schedule met?

1133. What could be done to improve the process?

1134. How well defined and documented were the Amazon Web Services AWS project management processes you chose to use?

1135. What is an Encumbrance?

1136. Were cost budgets met?

1137. What was learned?

1138. What were things that you need to improve?

1139. How well did the chosen processes fit the needs of the Amazon Web Services AWS project?

1140. Can the lesson learned be replicated?

1141. Will the Amazon Web Services AWS project deliverable(s) replace a current asset or group of assets?

1142. Did the Amazon Web Services AWS project management methodology work?

1143. Based on your Amazon Web Services AWS project communication management plan, what worked well?

5.1 Procurement Audit: Amazon Web Services AWS

1144. Are there regular reviews and analysis of the performance of the procurement function/unit?

1145. Is the purchasing department responsible for a continual review of marketing trends, particularly on long-term contracts and contracts containing escalation clauses?

1146. Was invitation to tender to each specific contract issued after the evaluation of the indicative tenders was completed?

1147. Is there no evidence of false certifications?

1148. Are there internal control systems in place to secure that laws and regulations are observed?

1149. Is the chosen supplier part of the organizations database?

1150. Are information technology resources (e-procurement) used to reduce costs?

1151. Does the strategy ensure that needs are met, but not exceeded?

1152. Did the additional works introduce minor or non-substantial changes to performance, as described in the contract documents?

1153. Are all purchase orders accounted for?

1154. Are requisitions and other purchase requests batched to reduce the number of orders issued?

1155. Is there no evidence of collusion between bidders?

1156. Are there procedures for trade-in arrangements?

1157. Is confidentiality guaranteed during the whole process?

1158. When such references were made, was a precise description of the performance not otherwise possible and were those references accompanied by the words or equivalent?

1159. Is it clear which procurement procedure the organization has opted for?

1160. When negotiation took place in successive stages, was this practice stated in the procurement documents and was it done in accordance with the award criteria stated?

1161. Is there a need for the procurement Amazon Web Services AWS project at all?

1162. Could bidders learn all relevant information straight from the tender documents?

1163. Are trial balances taken weekly for general ledgers for all funds?

5.2 Contract Close-Out: Amazon Web Services AWS

1164. How is the contracting office notified of the automatic contract close-out?

1165. Have all contract records been included in the Amazon Web Services AWS project archives?

1166. A change in circumstances?

1167. Have all contracts been completed?

1168. Have all contracts been closed?

1169. Parties: Authorized?

1170. Has each contract been audited to verify acceptance and delivery?

1171. How/When Used ?

1172. Why Outsource?

1173. Was the contract complete without requiring numerous changes and revisions?

1174. Are the signers the authorized officials?

1175. What is Capture Management?

1176. Parties: Who is Involved?

1177. What happens to the recipient of services?

1178. A change in knowledge?

1179. How does it work?

1180. A change in attitude or behavior?

1181. Was the contract type appropriate?

1182. Was the contract sufficiently clear so as not to result in numerous disputes and misunderstandings?

1183. Have all acceptance criteria been met prior to final payment to contractors?

5.3 Project or Phase Close-Out: Amazon Web Services AWS

1184. Were risks identified and mitigated?

1185. How much influence did the stakeholder have over others?

1186. Does the lesson educate others to improve performance?

1187. What are the marketing communication needs for each stakeholder?

1188. What hierarchical authority does the stakeholder have in the organization?

1189. Is there a clear cause and effect between the activity and the lesson learned?

1190. What Security Considerations needed to be addressed during the Procurement Life Cycle?

1191. When and how were information needs best met?

1192. What process was planned for managing issues/risks?

1193. What can you do better next time, and what specific actions can you take to improve?

1194. What is in it for you?

1195. Is the lesson significant, valid, and applicable?

1196. What were the desired outcomes?

1197. What advantages do the an individual interview have over a group meeting, and vice-versa?

1198. Complete Yes or No?

1199. Who controlled key decisions that were made?

5.4 Lessons Learned: Amazon Web Services AWS

1200. How effective was each Amazon Web Services AWS project Team member in fulfilling his/her role?

1201. How effective were the communications materials in providing and orienting team members about the details of the Amazon Web Services AWS project?

1202. Was there enough support – guidance, clerical support, training?

1203. How well do you feel the executives supported this Amazon Web Services AWS project?

1204. How well did the scope of the Amazon Web Services AWS project match what was defined in the Amazon Web Services AWS project Proposal?

1205. Is your organization willing to expose problems or mistakes for the betterment of the collective whole, and can you do this in a way that does not intimidate employees or workers?

1206. Recommendation: What do you recommend should be done to ensure that others throughout the organization can benefit from what you have learned?

1207. How clear were you on your role in the Amazon Web Services AWS project?

1208. Under what legal authority did the organization head and program manager direct the organization and Amazon Web Services AWS project?

1209. For the next Amazon Web Services AWS project, how could you improve on the way Amazon Web Services AWS project was conducted?

1210. Was the purpose of the Amazon Web Services AWS project, the end products and success criteria clearly defined and agreed at the start?

1211. To what extent was the evolution of risks communicated?

1212. What were the lessons learned on this Amazon Web Services AWS project?

1213. How was the Amazon Web Services AWS project controlled?

1214. Was the Amazon Web Services AWS project manager sufficiently experienced, skilled, trained, supported?

1215. What were the problems encountered in the Amazon Web Services AWS project-functional area relationship, why, and how could they be fixed?

1216. What things mattered the most on this Amazon Web Services AWS project?

1217. Who managed most of the communication within the Amazon Web Services AWS project?

1218. How efficient were Amazon Web Services AWS

project team meetings conducted?

1219. How well does the product or service the Amazon Web Services AWS project produced meet the defined Amazon Web Services AWS project requirements?

Index

ability 25, 63, 170, 176
abroad 111
absences 210
acceptable 46, 63, 120
acceptance 6, 100, 120, 122, 160, 190, 202, 229-230, 235-236
accepted 91
accepting 155
access 2, 9-10, 39, 41, 166, 170, 210
accomplish 8, 67, 101, 137, 208, 211, 219
accordance 234
according 30-31, 126
account 11, 31, 131-132
accounted 37, 234
accounting 132, 221
accuracy 43, 172, 217
accurate 10, 91, 121, 152, 217
achievable 89
achieve 8, 50, 58, 62, 88, 137, 166-167, 176, 193, 211, 224
achieved 18, 65, 89, 107, 226, 229
acquire 196
acquired 136, 166
across 43, 74, 199
action 75, 77, 106, 113, 118, 128, 132, 148, 167, 179
actionable 45
actions 21, 69, 85, 154, 170, 177, 179, 207, 237
active 113
actively 174
activities 23, 64, 75, 78, 112-113, 135-138, 145-146, 148, 150, 153, 156, 179, 185, 193, 204-205
activity 3-4, 25, 28, 113, 131, 135-139, 142-143, 147, 150, 152, 156-157, 194, 207, 237
actual 25, 120, 131-132, 153, 160, 168, 221, 227-228
actually 26, 58, 65, 73, 81, 133, 173, 224
adapted 113
addition 9, 87, 171
additional 34, 49, 51-52, 54, 159, 178, 181, 191, 207, 233
additions 76
address 20, 58
addressed 143, 174, 205, 210, 237
addressing 25, 88

adequate   128, 172, 191, 211
adequately   34, 38, 168, 189, 221
adopters   215
adoption   225
advance   209-210
advantage   50, 97
advantages   98, 121, 139, 238
advise 9
Advisory   198
affect 52, 54-55, 86, 117, 123, 126, 160, 163, 179, 198, 200, 210, 213, 222
affected   111, 134, 147, 172, 175
affecting   13, 20, 52, 114
affiliated   191
afford 177
against 32, 70-71, 126, 161-162, 204, 230
agencies   100, 111
agenda   209
agendas   97
agents 167
Aggregate   43
agreed   39, 41, 134, 172, 218, 240
Agreement   6, 92, 190, 209
agreements   223
agrees 91, 167
aiming 88
alerts   73
aligned   20
alignment   165
aligns   117
alleged   1
allocate   89
allocated   86, 168, 221
allocating   131, 169
allocation   131
allowances   209
allowed   93
allows 10, 152
almost 223
already   101, 197
altogether   181
always 10

243

Amazon   1-7, 9-15, 17-34, 36-48, 50-51, 53-68, 70, 72-90, 92-99, 101-121, 123, 125-139, 141, 143, 145-148, 150-164, 166, 168-176, 178-184, 186-188, 190-192, 194-198, 200-202, 204, 207-209, 211, 213, 215-219, 221, 223-225, 227, 229-235, 237, 239-241
-Amazon   77
ambitious   211
America   30
amount   162
amplify 52, 91
analysed   184, 205
analysing   183
analysis   3, 6, 12, 36, 38-44, 49-52, 60, 62, 66, 111, 116, 133, 145, 148, 154, 159, 170, 180-181, 184, 188, 200, 205, 211, 221, 233
analyze   2, 37, 41-44, 46, 48-49, 51, 63, 164, 181
analyzed   35-36, 38, 43, 45, 63, 73, 133
another   11, 95, 129, 137, 220
answer 12-13, 17, 24, 35, 48, 57, 69, 80
answered   23, 34, 47, 56, 68, 79, 104
answering   12, 228
anticipate   126
anyone   25, 101-102
anything   135, 144, 161, 203
appear   1, 194
applicable   13, 120, 203, 222, 227, 238
applied   71, 116, 138, 148, 169, 178
appointed   27-28
appraise   198
approach   44, 98, 156, 196, 211-212, 219-220, 225
approaches   59, 61, 174, 215
approval   28, 95, 120
approved   106, 119, 123, 160, 198, 200
approving   123, 199
Architects   8
archived   160
archives   235
arising 106
around 84, 215, 222
arriving 191
articulate   219
asking 1, 8, 160, 167
aspect 174
aspiration   220
assess 22, 182, 199

assessable   148
assessed   176
assessing   63, 74
Assessment   5-6, 9-10, 18, 120, 170, 172, 180, 191, 211, 213
assets 225, 231
assign 22
assigned   27, 29, 117, 126, 129, 133, 154, 186-187, 205, 207, 215
assigning   168
Assignment   4, 168
assist 62, 158, 203
assistant   8
associated   122, 182, 205
Assume   178
Assumption   3, 127
assurance   118, 170, 186, 191, 203
assure 43, 64
attainable   31
attained   177
attempted   25
attempting   73
attend 209
attendance   28
attendant   58
attended   28
attending   177
attention   13, 85
attitude   180, 236
attitudes   197
attributes   3, 94, 121, 137, 198-199, 225
audience   192-193
audited   172, 235
auditing   19, 71, 221
auditors   58, 225
auspices   9
author 1
authority   171, 176, 237, 240
authorized   132, 169, 235
automatic   235
available   17, 21, 28, 34, 38, 53-54, 82, 107, 132-133, 135-136, 141, 147, 156, 168, 172, 176, 178, 180, 182-183, 192, 225
Average   13, 23, 34, 47, 56, 68, 79, 104, 151, 203, 228
averse 225

Background   11, 109
backing   139
backward   200
balance   43
balances   234
bandwidth   227
barriers 43, 215
Baseline   4, 42, 126, 160
baselined   42, 172, 190
baselines   25, 34
basics 80
batched   234
Beauty 85
because   39, 41, 153
become   91, 94, 103, 119, 123, 202
before 10, 25, 70, 125, 142, 150, 155, 172, 182
beginning   2, 16, 23, 34, 47, 56, 68, 79, 104
begins 202
behavior   214, 236
Behaviors   44, 203
behaviours   193
belief   12, 17, 24, 35, 48, 57, 69, 80, 96
believable   89
believe 91, 96
beneficial   164
benefit 1, 18, 21, 66, 72, 133, 239
benefits   20, 53-54, 80, 83, 89-90, 121, 141, 177, 212
better 8, 33, 41, 46, 135, 150, 159, 177, 184, 202, 225, 230, 237
betterment   239
between   43, 46, 54, 123, 132-133, 155, 174, 195, 198, 215, 222, 234, 237
beyond   216
bidders   234
bidding   156
biggest   41, 61, 106, 187
blinding   52
Blokdyk   9
boards 58
bothered   215
bought 11
bounce   50, 53
boundaries   27
bounds   27

Breakdown 3-4, 66, 129, 145
briefed 27
brings 34
broader 220
broken 55
brought 98
budget 66, 72, 82, 115, 117, 132, 150, 152-154, 160, 172, 179, 186, 190, 195, 221, 227-228
budgets 101, 131-132, 168, 171, 221, 231
building 21, 75, 223-224
burden 202
burn-in 229
business 1, 8, 11, 18-20, 24-26, 29-30, 38, 46-48, 52, 54, 61, 70, 74, 85-86, 88-89, 91, 94, 98, 100-103, 117, 119, 128, 156, 160, 172, 180, 192, 200, 213, 222, 225, 229
busywork 106
button 11
buy-in 90, 230
calculate 141, 147, 164
calculated 222
called 106
cannot 156
capability 22, 41, 108, 172
capable 8, 24
capacities 86
capacity 21-22, 108, 113
capital 84
capture 45, 74, 127, 164, 235
captured 40, 81, 133, 187, 191
career 123, 171
careers 85
carried 184
cascading 43
category 30, 33, 131
caught 211
caused 1
causes 41, 48, 50, 54, 70, 114, 184
causing 20, 127
celebrate 207
celebrated 212
central 182
certain 67, 174
Certified 117, 186

chaired 9
challenge 8, 40, 203
challenged 85
challenges 99, 213
Champagne 9
champion 29
chance 185
chances 177
change 5, 17, 30, 48, 52, 59, 61, 66-67, 74, 80, 100, 102, 109-110, 120, 125, 129, 137, 160-161, 164, 167, 192-193, 198-201, 215, 218, 225, 235-236
changed 30, 81, 93, 101, 153, 157-158, 179, 221
changes 19, 38, 58, 64, 67, 70, 76, 82, 100, 108, 116, 118, 126, 128, 131-132, 134, 145, 172, 198-201, 221-222, 233, 235
Changing 84, 177
channels 122, 194, 218
chargeable 221
charged 221
Charter 2, 24, 29, 108, 115
charters 29
charting 154
charts 36, 42, 50
cheaper 41, 46
checked 71, 75, 78
checklist 9, 96
checks 225
choice 30, 33, 81
choose 12, 59
chosen 113, 194-195, 231, 233
circumvent 22
claimed 1
claims 226
classes 190
classified 169
clauses 233
cleaning 30
clearly 12, 17, 24, 27, 29, 32, 35, 48, 57, 69, 80, 121, 170, 172, 205, 240
clerical 239
client 9, 11, 39, 83, 229
clients 33
closed 73, 191, 201, 235
closely 11, 153

Close-Out   6-7, 235, 237
closest 84
Closing 6, 54, 231
Closings   38
Coaches   26, 29
cognizant   212
colleague   89
colleagues   97, 151
collect 44, 77, 158, 166, 207
collected   33-34, 44-45, 49, 52, 63, 147
collection   36-39, 42, 50, 166-167
collective   205, 239
college   60
collusion   234
combine   61
coming   49
command   75
commit   220
commitment   92, 113, 166, 168, 190
committed   33, 81, 128, 133, 173, 225
Committee   128
common   153, 156-157, 174
community   150, 158, 184
companies   1, 9, 202
company   8, 41, 46, 50, 85, 88-89, 91-92, 95, 102-103, 121, 151, 165, 222, 227
companys   227-228
compare   55, 67, 153, 221, 223
compared   86, 160, 162, 180, 186
Comparing   59
comparison   12
compatible   200, 219
compelling   25
competitor   222
complete   1, 9, 12, 23, 30, 133, 135, 137-138, 141, 148, 150-151, 154, 160, 164, 178, 235, 238
completed   13, 26, 31-33, 125, 142, 148, 150, 155, 207, 233, 235
completely   84, 150
completing   96, 129, 141
completion   28, 33, 60, 107, 114, 131-132, 142, 154, 160, 207, 224
complex   8, 42, 87, 128, 152, 223

complexity   35, 44, 186, 198
compliance   49
components   36, 42, 128, 152, 180
compute   13
computing   84
Concept   67, 167
concepts   128
Concern   171
concerns   21, 43, 84, 174, 227
concrete   219
condition   78
conditions   78, 98, 160, 207
conducted   68, 118, 172, 191, 199-200, 214, 225, 240-241
conducting   52
confidence   141, 165
confident   181
confirm   13
conflict 174, 199, 209-210
conflicts   122, 207
connected   153
connecting   98
consider   20, 22, 108, 137, 189
considered   18, 21, 38, 202
considers   49
consist 168
consistent   44, 77, 132
constantly   175
constitute   220
Constraint   3, 127
consultant   8, 156
consulted   102, 174
consulting   44
consults   51
consumers   101
contact   8, 118, 155
contacts   89
contain   19, 73, 115, 212
contained   1
containing   233
contains   9
content   32, 202
contents   1-2, 9
continual   11, 72-73, 233

continue 222
continuity 38
contract 6, 118, 131-132, 142, 155, 168-169, 189, 196, 208, 221, 233, 235-236
Contractor 6, 125, 147, 227
contracts 28, 131, 195, 227, 233, 235
contribute 205
control 2, 66, 69-71, 74-76, 107, 115, 120, 131-132, 158, 198-199, 202-203, 213, 220, 225, 233
controlled 53, 55, 221, 238, 240
controls 19, 54-55, 58, 60, 69-72, 77-78, 141, 178, 185, 226
convenient 39, 41
convention 100
converge 219
conversion 128, 222
convey 1
cooperate 158
Copyright 1
correct 35, 69, 152
correction 132
corrective 69, 118, 154
correspond 9, 11
cosmetic 128
costing 40, 222
counsel 188
counter 111
counting 94
countries 209
counts 94
course 30, 223
covering 76, 171
coworker 83
crashing 141
craziest 90
create 11, 18, 90-91, 98, 119, 125, 147, 165
created 51-52, 81, 110, 184, 191
creating 8, 41, 127
creativity 62
credible 158
crisis 20
criteria 2, 5, 9, 11, 27, 30-31, 33, 62, 74, 90, 93, 100, 105, 107, 120, 122, 124-125, 159, 162, 188, 190, 234, 236, 240
CRITERION 2, 17, 24, 35, 48, 57, 69, 80

critical 30, 32-33, 38, 52, 70, 78, 97, 102, 128, 154, 188, 212
criticism 51
criticized 211
Crosby 147
crucial 53
crystal 13
cultural 67
culture 28, 52, 170-171, 210
current 32, 35, 38, 46, 51, 54-55, 72, 89, 93, 96, 99-100, 131, 142, 190, 193, 231
currently 30, 132, 210, 213, 225
custom 22
customer 11, 18, 25, 31, 33-34, 45, 58, 71, 77, 81-82, 86-87, 89-90, 121, 157, 161, 177, 181, 183, 197, 229
customers 1, 18, 28, 31-32, 39, 41, 45, 51, 55, 82, 86-88, 91, 93, 99, 102, 122, 162, 164, 190
customize 192
cut-down 223
damage 1, 177, 182
Dashboard 9
dashboards 76
database 233
databases 166
day-to-day 72, 98, 140
deadlines 21, 92, 139
deceitful 83
decide 59, 162, 195, 204
decided 59, 207
deciding 95
decision 6, 50, 60-62, 66-67, 156, 202-203
decisions 60, 64, 73, 75, 78, 111, 172, 187, 202, 207-208, 210, 238
dedicated 8
deeper 13, 220
deepest 9
defect 41, 190
defects 47, 164, 199
define 2, 24, 28, 31, 33, 43, 53, 121, 129, 150, 203
defined 12-13, 17, 19, 24-32, 34-35, 47-48, 53, 55, 57, 69, 80, 125-126, 129, 133-134, 153-154, 164, 170, 172, 194, 231, 239-241
defines 19, 27, 30, 145
defining 8, 109, 191

definite 73
definition 127-128, 161, 194
degree 60, 211-212, 219-220
delays 135
delegate 210
delegated 24
deletions 76
deliver 18, 30, 58, 89, 95, 156, 159, 209
delivered 46, 90, 133, 152, 173, 208
delivers 145
delivery 21, 98-99, 139, 235
Delphi 195
demand 83, 180
demands 219
Deming 147
department 8, 91, 168, 197, 233
depend 196
dependent 99
depends 85
deploy 87
deployed 75
deploying 44
derive 74
Describe 19, 68, 123, 127, 139, 147, 199, 227
described 1, 125, 131, 160, 168, 201, 233
describes 226
describing 32
deserving 196
design 1, 9, 11, 30, 61, 65, 68, 75, 84, 104, 127, 180, 217
designed 8, 11, 49, 63-64, 68, 217
designing 8
desired 34, 58, 145, 161, 224, 238
detail 35, 44, 68, 130, 199
detailed 52, 55, 117, 131-132, 134, 136, 173, 186-187
details 192, 239
detect 78
detected 190
determine 11-12, 86, 92, 100, 113, 136, 158, 163, 190
determined 52, 86, 166-167, 182
determines 111
detracting 90
develop 57, 65, 67, 116, 120, 129, 179, 220

developed   9, 11, 27, 29, 31, 45, 60, 62, 127, 153, 166, 186, 193, 200, 205, 223-224
developer   181
developers   182
developing   55, 63, 132, 192
deviation   216
diagnose   182
Diagram   4, 54, 116, 141
diagrams   128, 154
dictates   153
Dictionary   3, 131
differ   195
difference   106, 133, 195
different   8, 26, 31, 54, 86, 114, 183, 194, 202
difficult 135, 137-138, 146
difficulty   183
dilemma   85
direct   131-132, 221, 240
direction   30, 41, 46
directions   184
directly 1, 51, 55, 111
Directory   6, 207
Disagree   12, 17, 24, 35, 48, 57, 69, 80
disaster   38, 153
discarded   100
discovered   63
discrete   168
discuss 147, 188
discussed   188, 203
discussion   43
display 42, 140
displayed   33, 36, 42, 50, 135, 150
disposed   160
disputes   236
disqualify   81
disruptive   48
Divided   23-24, 34, 47, 56, 68, 78, 104
division 115
Divisions   168
document   11, 30, 115, 118, 121, 126, 202, 207
documented   30, 45, 72, 74, 76-77, 118, 127-128, 133, 155, 163, 170-171, 194, 225, 230-231
documents   8, 152, 186, 210, 233-234

dollars 221
domain 39
domains 93
dominating 210
dormant 89
drawing 182
driving 89, 93
duplicate 163
Duration 4, 130, 147, 150, 184
durations 25, 152
during 30, 57, 106, 115, 143, 156, 176, 182, 185, 214, 234, 237
duties 198
dynamic 44
dynamics 25
earlier 93, 148
earned 6, 223-224
easily 125, 220
economic 182, 184
economical 96, 116
Economy 63, 111
eDiscovery 202
edition 9
editorial 1
educate 237
education 19, 74
effect 38, 181, 225, 237
effective 19, 83-84, 103, 188, 202, 204-206, 225-226, 239
effects 39, 112, 114, 139-140, 178, 208
efficiency 50, 77, 148, 189
efficient 196, 240
effort 37, 64, 97, 117, 131, 162, 169, 205, 217
efforts 25, 111, 155, 163
either 137
electronic 1, 189
element 132, 221-222
elements 11-12, 73, 86, 132, 166, 207, 222
Elevator 121
elicit 166
eliminated 163
e-mail 122
embarking 25
embody 204
emergent 44

emerging   21, 71
employee   59, 86, 227
employees   53, 86, 95, 99, 104, 226, 239
employers   110
empower   8
enable 48
enablers   82
encourage   62, 76, 189, 212
encouraged   168
end-users   225
engage   87, 190, 209, 212, 216, 220
engagement   45, 110, 175, 186
Enhance   72, 78
enhanced   85, 204
enlarged   182
enough   8, 85, 93, 99, 121, 123, 182, 211, 219, 239
ensure 25, 32, 58, 83, 94, 100, 103, 120, 128, 131, 148, 162-163, 166, 207, 212, 226, 233, 239
ensures   103
ensuring   10, 86, 205, 223-224
Enterprise   196
Entities 38
entity   1, 121
equipment   21, 107, 209, 225
equipped   28
equitably   24
equivalent   154, 234
errors   100, 128, 132, 156
escalated   172
escalation   233
essential   63
Essentials   98
establish   57, 158, 181
estimate   35, 38, 46, 150, 156, 188
estimated   28, 33, 38, 96, 116, 133, 158, 179, 227-228
estimates   4, 34, 42, 48, 117, 132-133, 147, 156, 161, 172
estimating   4, 117, 134, 150, 158, 173, 187
estimation   65
ethical 91, 218, 229
ethics   180
ethnic   91
evaluate   60, 67, 131, 134, 222
evaluated   161, 188

evaluating 62
evaluation 64, 73, 188, 214, 218, 233
events 43, 68, 131
everyday 54
everyone 25, 31, 167, 205, 209
everything 202
evidence 13, 39, 188, 196, 213, 233-234
evolution 35, 240
evolve 78
example 2, 9, 14, 21, 51, 70, 131, 211, 226
examples 8-9, 11
exceed 130, 153
exceeded 233
exceeding 45
excellence 8
excellent 41
except 132
excess 132, 221
exclude 64
execute 230
executed 38, 42, 160, 201
Executing 5, 155, 194
execution 115, 199, 208
executive 8, 90, 155, 190
executives 97, 239
existence 185
existing 11-12, 39, 41, 70, 94, 108, 126
exists 119, 142
expect 115, 150, 154
expected 20, 25, 94, 99, 113, 194, 202, 205, 218
expend 37
expense 132, 221
expenses 222
expensive 42, 135, 151
experience 84, 98, 104, 151, 176, 180, 205, 221, 227
experiment 101
Expert 9
expertise 61, 168, 225
experts 33, 147
expiration 142
explain 128, 163, 213
explained 11
explicitly 96

explore   54, 212, 219
expose 239
exposure   179
extent 12, 26, 65, 113-114, 205, 225, 240
external   25, 93
facilitate   12, 21, 76
facing 22, 85
factors 37, 40, 60, 90, 102, 109, 113, 158
failed 35
failing 87
failure 36, 104, 112, 184
failures 199
fairly   24
familiar 9
fashion 1, 27, 176
feasible   46, 49, 95, 158
feature 10
features   180, 230
feedback   2, 11, 25, 34, 36
figure   41
Filter   165
finalized   14
finally 120
financial   46, 48, 50, 53, 95, 139
fingertips   10
finish   136, 138-139, 141, 223
finished   139
fitness 226
flowery 119
flying   30
focused   44
follow 11, 72, 92, 96, 195, 229
followed   32, 117, 134, 186
following   9, 12, 167
follow-up   114, 156
for--and   71
forces 164
forecast   154, 224
Forecasts   154
forefront   96
foreseen   106
forever 101
forget 10

formal 6, 87, 134, 199, 219, 229-230
formally 28, 127, 133, 191, 221
format 11, 126, 207
formed 29, 33
forming 162
formula 13, 88
Formulate 24
formulated 116
forward 93, 104
foster 94, 100
framework 75, 85, 166
freaky 99
frequency 27, 71, 164, 167, 184
frequently 45-46, 210-212, 219-220
friction 212
friend 85, 89
frontiers 66
fulfill 106
fulfilling 239
full-blown 38
full-scale 65
fulltime 173
function 126, 156, 191, 229, 233
functional 116
functions 28, 53, 82, 103, 122, 170, 207, 219
funding 84, 93, 118, 178, 219
further 178
future 8, 45, 74, 213, 226
gained 51, 70, 73
gather 12, 35, 81
general 138, 190-191, 234
generally 196
generate 49-50, 63, 225
generated 55, 65, 132
generation 9
Gerardus 9
getting 127, 174, 203
glamor 30
global 63, 84
governance 94, 118, 171
governing 216
Graded 178
graphs 9, 36

gratitude 9
ground 43, 53
grouped 137
groups 86, 128, 134, 172, 192-193, 197
growth 52, 90, 139
guaranteed 32, 234
guidance 1, 239
guidelines 203
guides 115
Guiding 111
handle 143, 210
handled 119
handling 183
happen 22, 139, 185
happened 115
happening 85
happens 8, 11, 86, 88, 93, 118, 121, 133, 156, 158, 178, 213, 236
hardest 38
hardly 224
hardware 119
hazards 184-185
healthy 184
hearing 91
helpful 38
helping 8
high-level 26, 33
high-tech 94
hijacking 100
hinder 128
hiring 60, 76
historical 159
history 137, 145, 147
hitters 50
hitting 223
honest 91
housed 119
humans 8
hypotheses 48
identified 1, 22, 28, 31, 36, 39, 44, 46-47, 49, 54, 106, 118, 121, 126, 132, 137, 148, 154-155, 162, 170-171, 173, 176, 178-179, 184, 192, 203, 205, 210, 215, 221, 237
Identifier 108

identify 12, 17, 19, 21, 37, 41, 43, 49, 51-52, 112, 117, 125, 158, 168, 182, 193
ignoring 97
imbedded 70
immediate 43
impact 5, 28, 32, 35-37, 41-42, 46-47, 65, 102, 107, 149, 176, 178, 180, 182, 200-201, 208, 216-217, 222
impacted 192-193
impacting 152
impacts 151, 176
implement 21, 37, 69, 214, 217
implicit 84
importance 188, 212, 220
important 18, 40, 51, 55, 60, 84, 88, 90, 92, 97, 106, 111-113, 148, 164, 174, 225
improve 2, 11-12, 53, 57-61, 63-67, 108, 128, 145, 156, 163, 214, 231, 237, 240
improved 60-61, 65, 67, 77, 188
improving 57, 197
inaccurate 119
incentives 76
include 61, 64, 116-117, 119, 132
included 2, 9, 125, 128, 150, 158, 168, 198, 227, 235
includes 10, 36, 192
including 22, 24, 26, 31, 44, 46, 50, 58, 66, 73, 75, 77, 128, 206, 215
incomplete 119
increase 65, 91, 128, 148
increasing 98
incurrence 132, 221
incurring 221
in-depth 12
indicate 46, 78, 81, 90, 205
indicated 70
indicative 233
indicators 40, 46, 51, 55, 75, 114, 162-163
indirect 131-132, 169, 221
indirectly 1
individual 1, 41, 117, 136, 154, 219, 228, 238
industries 180
industry 81, 86, 92, 139, 149, 172
infected 184
infection 184

infinite 84
influence 66, 110, 112, 171, 202-203, 237
influences 210, 215
informal 219
informed 93, 107
ingrained 78
inhibit 67
initial 95, 153
initially 120
initiated 125, 159, 164, 201
initiating 2, 100, 106, 127
initiative 12, 108, 167, 175
Innovate 57
Innovation 50, 63, 73, 84, 100, 104, 140
innovative 98, 114, 159, 195
inputs 31-32, 54, 72, 147
insight 49, 53
insights 9
inspired 80
instead 89, 168
insurance 226
insure 104
insurers 58
integrate 77, 94, 114
Integrated 161
integrity 83, 201
intended 1, 62, 178
INTENT 17, 24, 35, 48, 57, 69, 80
intention 1
intentions 204-205
interact 82
interest 165, 174, 185, 197
interested 169
interests 37, 41, 169
interfaces 128
interim 92
internal 1, 25, 93, 98, 111, 225, 233
interpret 12-13
intervals 155, 190
interview 88, 238
intimidate 239
introduce 44, 181, 233
introduced 30

intuition 39
invaluable 2, 9, 11
inventory 157
investment 21, 166
investors 58
invitation 233
invoices 172
involve 99
involved 18, 53, 63, 95, 128, 134, 170, 173, 187, 192, 194, 197, 218, 235
involves 74
isolate 41
issued 233-234
issues 63, 108, 111, 122, 125-126, 134, 141, 143, 152, 168, 172, 186, 205, 208, 215, 237
Iterative 114
itself 1, 21
joining 126
jointly 212
journey 87
judgment 1, 204
justified 162
kicked 98
killer 98
knock-on 178
knowledge 11, 25, 36, 40, 51, 61, 69-70, 72-73, 76, 94-95, 97-98, 147, 171, 193, 204, 236
lacked 81
largely 51
latest 9
leader 19, 29, 50, 52
leaders 29, 31, 53, 87-88, 133, 215
leadership 30, 33, 63, 87, 113
learned 7, 73-74, 81, 231, 237, 239-240
learning 72-73, 132, 203-204, 214
ledgers 234
length 184
lesson 231, 237-238
lessons 7, 65, 74, 81, 239-240
letter 122
Leveling 137
levels 22, 28, 51, 55, 74, 81, 130, 166, 185
leverage 29, 63, 74, 84, 158

leveraged 25
Liability 1, 177
licensed 1
lifeblood 102
lifecycle 45
lifecycles 61
Lifetime 10
likelihood 62, 67, 179
likely 72, 89, 112, 161, 178, 203, 222
limited 11, 171
Linked 30, 203
Listed 1, 166
listen 94
logical 143
longer 75
long-term 70, 89, 104, 233
looking 217
losses 45
lowest 132, 141
magnitude 64
maintain 69, 83, 90
maintained 133, 148, 219, 221
makers 72, 156
making 19, 50, 61, 64, 66, 88, 167
manage 40, 53, 58, 83, 97, 108, 115-116, 120, 123, 134, 139, 156, 163, 168, 175, 180, 190, 208, 216
manageable 29
managed 8, 34, 126, 199, 240
management 1, 3-5, 11-12, 18, 21, 24, 26, 29, 36, 38, 40, 51, 58-59, 65-66, 73, 84, 97-98, 106, 115, 117-119, 125-128, 133-134, 147-148, 151, 153-155, 157, 160-163, 166, 171-172, 174, 176, 182-183, 186-187, 189-194, 196, 202, 204, 207, 213, 217-218, 221, 224-225, 230-232, 235
manager 8, 12, 17, 28, 32, 95, 108, 117-118, 186, 197, 229, 240
Managers 2, 105
manages 227
managing 2, 9, 105, 110, 205, 215, 237
mandatory 200
manner 132, 172, 187, 198, 229
manpower 131
mantle 97
manual 163

mapped 26
market 41, 139, 222-223
marketer 8
marketing 99, 101, 122, 127, 233, 237
material 131, 139, 164, 168, 222
materials 1, 125, 205, 209-210, 239
matrices 123
Matrix 3-5, 111, 123, 168, 182
matter 33, 40, 225
mattered 240
matters 203
maximizing 85
meaning 137
meaningful 37, 98, 212
measurable 31, 34, 157, 204, 211, 220
measure 2, 12, 18-19, 29-30, 35-37, 39-46, 49-50, 57-58, 61, 64, 66-67, 72-74, 77-78, 114, 126, 158-159, 162-165, 222
measured 22, 36-40, 42-46, 58, 70, 72, 169, 185
measures 39-40, 43-47, 49-51, 55, 75, 78, 114, 162, 195
measuring 132
mechanical 1
mechanics 198
mechanism 127, 198
mechanisms 166
medium 223
meeting 28, 40, 71, 125, 162, 166, 173, 175, 197, 204, 209-210, 225, 238
meetings 28, 32-33, 156, 177, 195, 203, 209, 241
megatrends 98
member 5-6, 30, 83, 145, 168, 174, 196, 213, 239
members 24, 26-27, 30, 32, 113, 119, 134, 148, 154, 173-174, 180, 187, 189, 207, 209-213, 216, 219-220, 226, 239
membership 211
memorable 212
message 192
messages 174
method 30, 38, 96, 151, 174-175, 183, 211, 225
methods 25, 27, 46, 116, 154, 159, 162, 180-181
metrics 4, 31, 41, 76, 109, 133-134, 164, 180, 193
milestone 3, 139-140, 160, 186
milestones 24, 110, 117, 138, 155
minimize 107, 217
minimizing 85

minimum 27, 227
minutes 28, 62, 210
missed 40, 91
Missing 100, 137
mission 49, 55, 83, 87, 90, 171, 219
mistakes 239
Mitigate 217
mitigated 177, 237
mitigating 155
mitigation 155, 181
modeling 51
models 53, 92, 101
modern 147
modified 65
moments 53
momentum 82, 91
monetary 18, 218
monitor 62, 72-73, 75, 78, 158
monitored 73, 106, 147, 150
monitoring 6, 72, 75, 77, 126, 143, 154, 217
monthly 131, 221
months 61-62, 160
motivation 71, 109
motive 167
movement 147
moving 104
multiple 180, 214
myself 100
narrative 127
narrow 54
national 113, 184
nature 44
nearest 13
nearly 91
necessary 44, 53, 55, 61, 74, 82, 92, 98, 131, 158, 161, 176, 189, 207
needed 21-22, 31, 54, 64, 70-71, 75, 114, 117, 154, 156, 159, 186, 237
negative 111, 152
negotiate 83
negotiated 92
neither 1
Network 4, 141, 215

Neutral 12, 17, 24, 35, 48, 57, 69, 80
nominated 192
normal 78, 132, 184
Notice 1
notified 192, 199, 235
number 23, 34, 47, 56, 68, 78, 92, 104, 137, 148, 163, 210, 234, 242
numerous 235-236
objective 8, 36, 125, 157, 161, 182, 203
objectives 18, 20, 24, 29-30, 49, 55, 74, 77, 88, 90, 95, 103, 117, 154, 160, 162, 173-174, 178-179, 197, 205, 208, 211, 220
observed 58, 233
obsolete 98
obstacles 22, 111, 159
obtain 229
obtained 34, 43, 120
obvious 104
obviously 13
occurrence 199
occurring 64, 106
occurs 20, 70, 195, 218
offerings 55, 67
Office 106, 196, 235
officials 235
one-time 8
ongoing 45, 59, 72, 150, 225
on-going 118
online 11
on-site 207
operate 184
operates 92
Operating 6, 77, 131, 209
operation 78
operations 12, 76-78
operators 72
opponent 203
opponents 215
opposed 174
opposite 92, 96
opposition 98
optimal 62, 66, 189, 227
Optimize 66, 78
optimized 90

option 81
options 17, 178
orders 234
organized 137, 148, 214
organizm 184
orient 71
orienting 239
original 22, 203
originate 73
others 153, 158-160, 165, 171, 174, 177, 186, 198, 202, 220, 237, 239
otherwise 1, 67, 160, 204, 234
outcome 13, 112, 119, 145, 208
outcomes 42-43, 59, 63, 78, 99, 114, 159, 178, 224, 238
outlier 137
outlined 74
output 29, 42, 78
outputs 32, 54, 72, 114, 143, 206
outside 62, 100, 107, 156, 210
Outsource 195, 235
outsourced 147
outweigh 177
overall 12-13, 20, 77, 86, 106, 128, 188, 203, 227
overcome 159
overhead 131-132, 168, 221-222
overheads 118
overlooked 107, 217
Oversight 125, 213
overtime 143
owners 129
ownership 32, 69
package 131
packages 168
Panels 206
paragraph 99
parallel 142
parameters 70
Pareto 50, 154
parking 187
particular 38, 51, 204, 217
Parties 235
partners 18, 85-87
pattern 138

paycheck 102
paying 85
payment 172, 236
pending 201
people 8, 22, 41, 51, 63-64, 73, 75-76, 82, 84-86, 88-89, 94, 96, 98, 127, 168, 177-178, 180, 182, 187, 194, 196, 209, 223
perceived 212
percent 93, 95
percentage 123
perception 60-61, 91
perform 22, 24-25, 27, 120, 185, 198, 229
performed 59, 123, 131, 135-136, 177
performing 106, 179, 188-189
perhaps 223
period 63, 132, 156, 179
periodic 187
periods 199
permission 1
permit 44
person 1, 140, 169
personal 225
personally 123
personnel 18, 73, 167, 186, 205
pertaining 180
pertinent 73
phased 132
phases 45, 138
picked 96
planet 73, 75
planned 38, 42, 70, 74, 78, 107, 120, 135, 179, 237
planners 73
planning 3, 9, 73, 77, 109, 113-114, 125, 131, 142-143, 153, 169, 197, 204-205, 218
Planning- 70
Pocket 150
Pockets 150
points 23, 34, 47, 56, 68, 78, 104, 166-167
poking 149
policies 81, 170, 180
policy 29, 72, 118, 128, 143, 178
Political 67, 101, 139
population 113
portfolio 99, 194

portfolios 175
portion 152
portray 50
positioned 158
positive 61, 91, 193
possess 211, 225
possible 35, 37, 50, 54, 63, 65, 69, 81, 84, 148, 150, 190, 234
post-test 214
potential 18, 27, 37, 43, 60, 62, 64, 81-82, 98, 121, 168, 177, 185, 210, 215, 218
practical 49, 57, 66, 69, 196-197
practice 42, 204, 234
practices 1, 11, 74, 76, 134, 225, 230
preaward 189
precaution 1
precede 141
precise 234
predict 78, 199
Predictive 145
pre-filled 9
Premium 176
prepare 167, 171, 175, 188
prepared 156
preparing 153
present 45, 74, 120, 183, 212
presented 207
presenting 210
preserve 28
pressures 139
prevent 45, 118, 127, 132, 210
prevents 19
previous 25, 227
previously 200
prices 189
primary 109, 134
printing 9
priorities 39, 43, 160
priority 137, 212, 220
privacy 115
problem 17, 20, 24-26, 31, 50-51, 111, 120-121, 190, 196, 199, 223

problems   17, 19-22, 41, 64-65, 67, 70, 86, 114, 166, 218, 239-240
procedure   148, 205, 234
procedures   11, 72, 74, 76-77, 127, 132, 134, 143, 153, 155-156, 162-164, 166, 186, 190, 203, 234
proceed   169
proceeding   150
process   1-6, 8, 11, 26-27, 29, 31-33, 36, 41-43, 46-47, 49-55, 58, 60-62, 65, 69-74, 76-78, 106, 113, 115, 123, 125-126, 128, 143, 147, 151, 155, 162-163, 166-167, 176, 180, 182-183, 188, 190, 194, 198, 202, 207-208, 213, 217, 223-227, 230-231, 234, 237
processes   26, 38, 45, 48-50, 52-53, 55, 70, 73, 76, 111, 113, 133, 163, 194-195, 200, 226, 230-231
produce   113, 143, 156, 194, 196
produced   61, 241
producing   123
product   1, 11, 38, 51, 55, 98-99, 108, 118, 120, 126, 139, 153, 161, 164, 176-177, 181, 195-197, 208, 215, 223-225, 230, 241
production   59
products   1, 20-21, 41, 103, 113, 120, 123, 156, 161, 190, 197, 219, 240
Profession   177
profile 205
Profitably   78
profits 160
program   20, 60, 171, 204, 213, 215, 217, 225, 240
programme   195
programs   58, 149, 175, 196
progress   27, 42, 67, 77, 88, 104, 113, 126, 158, 167, 190, 204
prohibited   132
project 2-4, 6-9, 19-20, 22, 31, 38, 51, 53, 74, 76, 84, 87, 95-97, 99, 101, 103-120, 123, 125-130, 132-138, 140-141, 145-148, 150-155, 157-161, 163, 169-173, 175-176, 178-179, 182-183, 186-187, 190-191, 194-197, 200-201, 207-208, 215-219, 223-225, 227, 229-232, 234-235, 237, 239-241
projected   131
projects   2, 93, 100, 105, 112-114, 123, 126, 129, 148, 175, 179-181, 183, 190, 194, 196-197, 207, 223-224
promising   98
promote   41, 51
promptly   172
proofing   58

properly	11, 26, 31, 38, 106-107, 121, 169
property	205
proponents	215
Proposal	188, 239
proposals	73
proposed	21, 36, 63-64, 116, 120, 189, 227-228
Propriety	218
protect	55, 94, 115
protected	209
protection	85, 177
protocols	163
proved	230
provide	20, 53, 95, 102-103, 110, 122, 131, 142, 152, 159, 164, 217, 220-222
provided	9, 13, 76, 128, 188, 191, 209
provides	140, 169
providing	110, 152, 161, 239
provision	117, 202
Public	186
publisher	1
pulled	93
purchase	9, 11, 189, 234
purchased	11
purchasing	233
purpose	2, 11, 83, 158, 168, 191, 212, 219-220, 240
purposes	109
pursued	100
pushing	99
qualified	24, 187
qualifying	152
quality	1, 4, 6, 11, 38, 42-43, 49, 51, 71, 107, 111, 114, 118, 126, 147, 152, 154, 162-164, 166-167, 170-171, 186, 191, 203-204
question	12-13, 17, 24, 35, 48, 57, 69, 80, 92, 111, 166, 209, 215
questions	8-9, 12, 49, 119, 206
quickly	12, 50-51, 53
quotes	189
radically	48
ranking	199
rather	44, 93, 222
Rating	188, 213
rational	132
rationale	202, 222

reaching   103
reaction   214
reactivate   89
readiness   191
readings   75
realism 188
realistic   115, 131, 211
reality 161
realized   83, 229
really   8, 21
reason 88, 96
reasonable   83, 116-117, 133, 172
reasons   25
reassess   117
re-assign   137
rebuild 98
receive   9-10, 28, 46, 99, 174, 193, 208
received   27, 90, 186
receives   213
receiving   205
recently   11, 90
recipient   236
recognize   2, 17-20, 65
recognized   18, 20, 60, 172, 174, 204
recognizes   17
recommend   85, 89, 125, 239
record 166, 209
recorded   162, 222
recording   1
records   19, 54, 148, 221, 235
recovery   38
Recurrence   185
redefine   30, 33
re-design   55
reduce 179, 202, 233-234
reduced   184
reducing   71, 98
Reduction   214
references   234, 242
reflect 51, 127
reform 40, 73, 95
reforms 21, 36, 46
regarding   102, 119, 156, 188-190, 197

Register 2, 5, 110, 174, 178-179
regret 62
regular 27, 33, 227, 233
regularly 28, 30, 32, 156, 226
regulation 213
regulatory 208
relate 147-148, 200
related 42, 44, 76, 119, 160, 170, 175, 198-199, 224
relation 19, 83, 111
relations 77, 93
relative 77, 212, 220
relatively 87
releases 227
relevant 11, 31, 38, 53, 75, 102-103, 114, 192, 208, 234
reliable 28, 184
remaining 152, 158
remedial 45
remedies 43
Remember 151
remotely 168
remove 63
remunerate 59
repair 190
repeat 113
rephrased 11
replace 108, 231
replaced 114
replicate 163
replicated 231
Report 5-6, 44, 75, 140, 165, 196, 207, 219, 227
reported 119, 132, 154, 216, 223
reporting 71, 119, 147, 164
reports 46, 110, 118, 162, 168, 186, 199
represent 58, 161
reproduced 1
reputation 95, 102
request 5, 49, 160-161, 198-201
requested 1, 64, 200
requests 198-199, 234
require 38, 70, 143, 152, 213
required 21, 25, 31, 34, 64-65, 118, 135-136, 141, 148, 166, 193, 217, 225-226
requires 107

requiring 110, 235
research 98, 139, 206
Reserve 157
reserved 1
reserves 221
reside 209
resilient 192
resolution 53, 125, 174
resolve 138, 207, 209
resolved 152, 172, 176
Resource 4-5, 9, 120, 131, 133, 138, 143, 145, 147, 169, 172, 191, 197
resourced 205
resources 2, 9, 21, 28, 34, 43, 64, 66, 76, 78, 81, 84, 86, 89, 107, 117, 128, 133, 136-137, 141, 145, 148, 154, 158, 168, 191, 207, 209, 216, 219, 233
respect 1
respective 114
respond 179
responded 13
responding 178
response 20, 70, 73, 75, 78, 228
responses 205
responsive 150, 158
restrict 121
result 54, 58, 61, 126, 159-160, 175, 193, 200, 236
resulted 71, 213
resulting 53, 114
results 9, 25, 30, 44, 55, 57-59, 62, 64-65, 67, 75-76, 113, 137, 147, 156, 159, 162, 166, 194, 213-214
retain 80, 102, 163
retrospect 93
return 39, 61, 141, 166
returned 30
revenue 41, 46
review 11-12, 120, 156, 199, 202, 233
reviewed 27, 127, 155, 163, 190
reviewer 211
reviews 11, 118, 177, 233
revised 48, 71, 185
revisions 235
reward 41, 52, 196
rewards 76

rights   1
routine 70
rushing 175
safely   226
safety   103, 116, 225
samples   163
sampling   154, 162
satisfied   100, 156, 229
satisfies 223
satisfying   87
savings 34, 48
scenarios   199
schedule   3-4, 30, 38, 66, 72, 101, 116, 122, 133-134, 142, 147, 152-155, 160, 169, 172-173, 179, 187, 200, 207, 222, 227, 231
scheduled   119, 133, 156, 188, 190
Schedules   126, 131, 152-153, 179, 188
scheduling   134, 172-173, 187
scheme   73
Science   151
Scientific   151
scopes 125
Scorecard   2, 13-15, 195
scorecards   76
Scores 15
scoring 11
Screen 198
screening   226
scripts 128
seamless   104
second   13
secondary   134
section 13, 23, 34, 47, 56, 68, 78-79, 104
sector 223
secure 97, 233
Securing   45, 97
security   19, 72, 110, 128, 182, 201, 237
segment   192
segmented   31
segments   31, 86, 222
select   49, 77
selected   57, 62, 115-116, 158-159, 180, 182
selecting   93, 190
Selection   5, 188

sellers 1
selling 86, 202
senior 87, 97, 211
separated 169
sequence 148
sequencing 95, 113
series 12
Serious 119, 177
service 1-2, 8-9, 11, 38, 60-61, 81, 88, 98, 126, 139, 178, 196-197, 241
Services 1-7, 9-15, 17-34, 36-48, 50-51, 53-68, 70, 72-90, 92-99, 101-121, 123, 125-139, 141, 143, 145-148, 150-164, 166, 168-176, 178-184, 186-188, 190-192, 194-198, 200-202, 204, 207-209, 211, 213, 215-219, 221-225, 227-237, 239-241
session 153
setbacks 50, 53
setting 221
several 9
severely 55
shared 73, 159, 203
sharing 72, 220, 222
shortest 148
short-term 220
should 8, 21, 26, 37, 44, 46, 49, 52, 59-61, 65, 67, 74, 76-77, 83, 85, 87, 91, 94, 106-107, 110, 113, 115, 119, 125, 132, 136, 140, 145, 150, 156, 164, 167, 171, 176, 179-180, 183, 188, 192, 200, 207-208, 217-218, 239
showing 113
signature 103
signatures 143
signed 125
signers 235
signing 162
similar 25, 31, 50, 55, 67, 137, 145, 216
simple 87, 211, 220, 223
simply 9, 11, 202
single 99, 156, 214, 222
single-use 8
situation 18, 35, 157, 178, 223
skeptical 101
skilled 240
skills 22, 39, 41, 44, 83, 94-95, 148-149, 172, 178, 193, 204, 217, 220, 226

smallest   20, 61
social   99, 101, 184
software   21, 119, 133, 153, 176, 183, 192, 194, 227
solicit   25
soliciting   210
soluiton   227
solution   42, 49, 53, 57-58, 61-66, 69, 128, 227
solutions   38-39, 41, 57, 59-60, 62-63, 65, 67, 178
Someone   8
someones   211
something   91, 115, 160, 182
Sometimes   38
Source 5, 84, 184, 188
sources   50, 54, 63, 81, 182, 210
special 9, 76, 108, 189, 192
specific   9, 21, 29, 31, 34, 96, 128, 135, 137-138, 143, 146, 154, 157, 163, 180, 192, 197, 200, 233, 237
specified   103, 184
specify 219
Speech   121
spoken 90
sponsor   18, 229
sponsored   29
sponsors   18, 156, 211
stability 43, 126
staffed 34
staffing 22, 76, 133
stages   117, 234
standard   8, 143, 222, 227
standards   1, 11-12, 78, 103, 127, 155, 163-164, 166-167, 200, 221
started 9, 139, 142
starting 12, 114
startup 96, 108
stated 93, 96, 234
statement   3, 12, 65, 67, 94, 125
statements   13, 23-24, 31, 34, 47, 51, 56, 68, 79, 104, 119, 125, 166
static   199
status   5-6, 51, 107, 133, 155, 186, 190, 196, 207, 215, 223-224, 227
statute 213
statutory   208

steering	128, 155, 190
storage	166
straight	234
strategic	77, 88, 108, 117
-Strategic	73
strategies	98, 155, 181, 192, 202-203, 205, 214, 225
strategy	20, 59, 64, 75, 86, 89, 99, 113, 162, 178, 192, 203, 226, 233
strengths	230
strong	170
stronger	95
Strongly	12, 17, 24, 35, 48, 57, 69, 80, 198-199
structure	3-4, 66, 87, 94, 129, 145, 154, 183, 189
stubborn	83
stupid	87
subject	9-10, 33, 120
subjective	119
submit	11
submitted	11, 200
submitting	165
subset	20
succeed	85, 211
success	18, 30, 35-37, 39-40, 58, 67, 70, 88, 90, 98, 100, 102, 104, 106, 112, 125, 128, 176-177, 187, 193, 196, 203, 240
successful	52, 58, 78, 90, 99, 101, 103, 106-107, 145, 161, 196
successive	234
sufficient	35, 183
suggest	205, 215
suggested	69, 161
suitable	36, 208
supervisor	170
supplied	225
supplier	82, 233
suppliers	32, 53, 55, 87, 190
supplies	229
Supply	88
support	8, 50, 61, 69, 78, 97-98, 103, 118, 122, 131, 143, 171-172, 192, 203-205, 213, 228, 239
supported	33, 51, 113, 182, 239-240
supporting	65, 134, 166
supportive	170-171
supports	213
supposed	205

surface 70
Surveys 9
SUSTAIN 2, 66, 80
Sustaining 70, 111
symptom 17
system 11-12, 49, 73, 84, 87, 121-122, 125, 127, 131-132, 145, 171, 201, 203-206, 221-225
systematic 36, 44
systems 36, 44, 50, 52, 58, 76, 93, 111, 190, 192, 204, 224, 230, 233
tables 128
tackled 85
tactics 202-203
Taguchi 147
tailor 192
taking 41, 46, 113, 196, 210
talents 94
talking 8
target 32, 113, 165, 192
targets 157, 205, 223
tasked 69
taxation 225
Teaches 51
teaching 204
teamed 210
teaming 209
technical 61, 67, 113, 121, 128, 147, 149, 199
technique 38, 195
techniques 51, 53, 92, 116, 148, 181
technology 81, 98, 139, 176, 182-183, 209, 233
templates 8
tender 233-234
tenders 233
Test-Cycle 167
tested 19, 65, 106
testing 62, 121, 162, 180, 225
thankful 9
themes 212
themselves 44, 82, 95, 220
theory 71
therefore 184
things 68, 96, 125, 156, 181, 183, 217, 231, 240
Thinking 49, 62, 84, 104

thorough 200
thoroughly 126
thought 215
threat 88
threats 127, 185
through 49, 87, 125, 180, 198, 211
throughout 1, 127, 147-148, 239
tighter 101
time-based 169
time-bound 31
timeframe 158
timeline 117, 164, 200
timely 27, 172, 176, 187, 198, 208, 210
Timescales 139
timing 208, 214
todays 147
together 98
tolerable 185
tolerances 216
tolerated 135
tomorrow 73, 75, 102
top-down 75
topics 61
toward 71, 196
towards 53
traced 128, 161
tracked 118, 125, 186, 198
tracking 26, 77, 126, 154, 172
traction 101
trade-in 234
trademark 1
trademarks 1
tradeoff 189
trade-offs 155
trained 26, 31, 33, 180, 189, 240
training 21-22, 67, 74, 76, 115, 148, 171, 192, 196, 205, 209, 213-214, 239
Transfer 13, 23, 34, 47, 56, 68-69, 76, 79, 104, 227
translated 34
travel 209
trends 21, 51, 55, 184, 233
Tricky 89
triggered 133

triggers 191
trophy 97
trouble 102
trying   8, 52, 100-101, 193
ubiquitous   84
ultimate   93
unable 209
underlying   60, 132
undermine   101
understand   33, 107, 153, 182-183
understood   90, 93, 121, 205
undertake   49
underway   64
uninformed   93
uniquely   215
Unless   8
unplanned   210
unresolved   119, 143
update   152, 160
updated   9-10, 51, 118, 131, 187
updates   10, 76, 133, 147, 227
upload 209
usability   85
useful   57, 71, 130, 156
usefully 12, 20
UserID   140
utility   151
utilizing 65
validate   224
validated   26-27, 33, 55
Validation   224
valuable   8
values 87, 184
variables   42, 52, 78, 213
Variance   6, 211, 221
-variance   154
variances   154, 169, 186, 222
variation   17, 25, 36, 42, 50, 54, 71
variety 64
various 117
Vendor 107, 118, 142, 172
vendors   20, 83, 134
verbally   168

verbiage 218
verified 10, 26-27, 33, 55
verify 74, 77, 152, 160, 163, 223, 235
version 227, 242
versions 26, 31
versus 120
vested 185
vetting 128
viable 129
vice-versa 238
violate 128
Virgin 30
vision 87, 94, 171
visits 118
visualize 135, 150
voices 110
volatile 63
volatility 180
warning 133
warrant 207
warranty 1, 199
weaknesses 127, 188, 230
wealth 39, 41
weekly 234
whether 8, 74, 95, 204
-which 174
widgets 160
willing 164, 177, 181, 239
wishes 204
within 49, 63, 135, 137, 150-151, 165, 171, 184, 197, 200, 213, 240
without 1, 13, 42, 90, 98, 114, 131, 152, 200, 235
worked 66, 106, 187, 216, 232
workers 91, 239
workflow 203
workforce 22, 86-87
working 62, 70, 74, 113, 128, 169, 171, 180, 202
Worksheet 4, 150, 158
writing 11, 119, 123, 168
written 1, 205
year-end 131
yourself 54, 83

Lightning Source UK Ltd.
Milton Keynes UK
UKHW02f2031081018
330218UK00005B/44/P